YOURU

(Pronounced you-ru)

YOURU

(Pronounced you-ru)

Find the Guru within You

SARAH SUSAK

Published in 2025 by Sarah Susak
sarahsusak.com
@sarah_susak

Copyright © Sarah Susak, 2025

Interior images: p.29 Shutterstock; p.156 Freepik
Book cover image: Katie Kaars Photography

The right of Sarah Susak to be identified as the author of this work has been asserted in accordance with the Copyright, Design and Patents Act, 1988

All rights reserved. No part of this publication may be reproduced, stored in a retrieval system, or transmitted in any form or by any means, electronic, mechanical, photocopying, recordng or otherwise, without prior permission of the publisher.

The events depicted within this work have been recollected to the best of the author's ability. The names and identifying details of certain individuals have been changed to protect their privacy.

Edited by Rachel Ramaekers
Cover design by Halan Susak
Typeset by Lorena Susak

 A catalogue record for this book is available from the National Library of Australia

ISBN: 978 1 76381 519 3 (Paperback)

To the one who created me, Judes.
To the one who created us, Halan.
To the one we created together, Stella.

Contents

Preface ix

Prologue xvii

Introduction 1

Part One: Guru 11

    Chapter One: Guru Parents 13

    Chapter Two: Guru Partner 35

    Chapter Three: Guru Society 53

    Chapter Four: Guru Job 73

    Chapter Five: Guru Doctors 91

    Chapter Six: Guru Beauty 137

    Chapter Seven: Guru Spiritual Leader 147

Part Two: Youru 169

    Chapter Eight: Are You Medi? 171

    Chapter Nine: Youru 187

    Chapter Ten: Comm-Unity 205

    Chapter Eleven: From Drama to Dharma 219

Epilogue 232

Afterword 233

The Treasure Chest 236

About The Author 244

Every single day, I try a bit harder than the day before to realise my own deserving power, my own self-worth, independent of anyone or anything else.

You deserve the best.
Never feel unworthy or
not justified in having the best.
I tell you, this is your heritage,
but you have to accept it.
You have to expect it.
You have to claim it.
To do so is not demanding too much.

– Guru Deva, Swami Brahmananda Saraswati –

Preface

One day you will tell your story of how you have overcome what you are going through now, and it will become part of someone else's survival guide.

– Unknown –

We have not met, but I can assure you that throughout the earlier years of my life, said no one ever, *oh, I wish so much that I could be exactly like Sarah. She's so independent, so in control, so calm and just eternally happy.* I was certifiably mad. I would break out my defensive armoury at the deliverance of any words that even remotely sounded like criticism. If Desperate Debbie had a twin sister, it would have been me. I literally thought I might die if I was not in a relationship. I needed validation and compliments as often as the average human needs to go to the toilet. I lived for the day that a cosmetics manufacturer would produce an innovative sensitive skin cream, not to deal with rashes but that I could have rubbed all over my pathetic body to help reduce the amount I would cry if I saw something sad or someone didn't like me. If you saw me leave a shopping mall with all my bags in tow you would have been forgiven for thinking I had just swallowed a bag of amphetamines, I was on such a retail high. And you only had to fail to answer your phone twice before I would have mentally determined that you had been in a life-taking car accident and that I would never see you again, such was the epic nature of my ability to catastrophise.

It is undeniably true that I have lived most of my life (and my pursuit for personal fulfilment) entirely reliant on people, places or phenomena "out there" to make me happy and feel worthy. But the whack from the wrecking ball that was a life-threatening cancer diagnosis just one year after I had given birth to my first (and only) child was of such a vibratory magnitude that I was catapulted onto a new path. A path as terrifying as it was radically liberating. A path that not only offered me a way to move this new mountain of grief, fear and anxiety entirely out of the way but also left me with no other choice but to take that mountain assigned to me and find a way to show others that it can be moved.

I am not trying to change you, only myself

> *If each of us would only sweep our own doorstep, the whole world would be clean.*
>
> – Mother Theresa –

This book is certainly not about proselytising. I am not trying to convert you from where you stand today in your own worldview to my own. Think of my stories as the underground and yourself as the miner, digging out any useful insights that may be valuable and applicable to your own personal discoveries. I am fully cognisant of the fact that I cannot change you. It would be a fruitless and, in fact, manipulative exercise to try to do so. I don't desire to change you at all. I do, however, want you to believe and know that you can change yourself *if you wish to*. In fact, that is where your power lies. And if this book inspires you do that for yourself, I would be happy.

Almost as painfully repetitive as an old locked vinyl groove, I have on many occasions found myself stuck in a continuous loop of the same questions. Some of these may sound familiar.

Why is life so hard sometimes? Why do good people suffer? What is wrong with this crazy world? And the most agonising of all: How can I change it? Far too often my first instinct has been to place all of my effort and energy into trying to change the people and situations around me. Clearly under a mistaken belief that if those changes happened, then just like magic, things would be better and I would be eternally happy. However, if you have tried that for as many years and as many times as I have, I am sure you will agree that it's really exhausting. The benefits are always only fleeting before a new challenging person or circumstance will pop up and threaten the new-found peaceful existence again.

So, in recent times, I have shifted to focusing on sweeping up my own mess: sorting out what is making me afraid or unhappy and addressing that for myself, lasering in on my own self-care and healing. Through that individual reform, from that expanded happier state of consciousness, I am hoping that, taken out into the world, it might have some kind of beneficial ripple effect on the collective. I have ultimately found it both less intimidating and more fruitful to just start with the crap that is on my own doorstep and seek to establish a happy home within. Any natural and broader impact on others is then a happy and welcome by-product of my own self work.

I am not an expert, but I am on a path

I have been a lifetime devotee to a charitable organisation in Sydney called the Wayside Chapel, which I talk a lot about in Chapter Ten. It was here, in this beautiful protective sanctum of real community, that I learned one of my most important life lessons. I learned that the goal in life and in all relationships should never be about establishing yourself as an expert anyway. And that to do so is actually the antithesis of what it means to create meaningful human connections. Because of course, as soon as you do that, it makes the "other" somehow inferior to you. And that is quite literally the last thing I wish to do by writing this book. The old pastor of the Wayside Chapel, Rev. Graham Long AM, taught all of us lucky enough to be in his presence that people are not problems to be solved, they are people to be met. And that if we can truly meet each other without that dividing layer of superiority, then real and genuine movement, progression and healing can take place.

I have come to believe that there is actually a real danger in pedestals. They separate people from each other. If they are too high, you can fall off them and really hurt yourself. If someone kicks one out from under you, also not good. And if you crane your neck too high to stare in awe at someone you yourself have placed on one, you will for sure, at some point, need to see a chiropractor for that injury too. And besides, sometimes I wonder whether some people even want to be placed on these pedestals at all. I am sure there is a real pain and pressure experienced in that. Those exalted by others, or even those who freely exalt themselves, can also be fragile, fallible and afraid, and we need to never lose awareness of that, or else hatred and anger become separating forces in our lives.

Bottom line is that I do not wish to write a book that makes you feel shit about yourself. I want you to feel comfortable with and enjoy your own pace and journey. I am deliberately avoiding deducing my personal stories into some kind of guaranteed methodology or an unrealistic "top ten things"-type manifesto. I am also not positioning myself as an expert who can teach you, especially when I now know (and I will show you how I know) that you actually already have all that you need to teach yourself.

So, what the heck am I doing then?

I am a researcher. I am a storyteller. I am a share bear.

> *To know even one life has breathed easier because you have lived. This is to have succeeded.*
>
> – Ralph Waldo Emerson –

I have lived my entire life in what, until now, has felt like a somewhat insatiable search for *the way*. I was born with a thirst for sipping solutions. With a tenacious unwillingness to allow the cup to stay empty for too long, constantly refilling it with new knowledge or new ways to satisfy my thirst for the answers. I have been out there since I was very young, relentlessly pounding the pavement, obsessively doing the research, enthusiastically exploring all the different ways, worshipping every possible being or idea outside of myself in hope of the answers.

I have, of course, stagnated at so many points along the way, but for the first time in my life I have never felt as close to understanding what it is that I need to do. I finally feel like everything I need to know is now within my reach. That I can do less searching and more being. I feel like the answers are less of an illusory mirage that I am uselessly clutching at and more of an actual, experienced and verifiable truth. That, funnily enough, I don't even have to do anything to reach out and touch them, because they are already within me.

So, this is me not wanting to keep that shit to myself. This is me offering up the fruits of a lifelong labour. This is me hoping that from reading my stories just one person is able to feel a little more able to cope for themselves, a little less helpless, a little less reliant on other people or things. I believe in the power of communal sharing and storytelling for inspiration. In deciding to write this book, I wondered: if I was willing to share my own stories, would that create an open and safe space for people to feel courageous enough to look at, or also share, their own? Would someone who was about to experience something I have already, or something remotely similar, benefit from hearing from someone who has navigated their way through it? Could my own personal hindsight give someone a head-start on their own efforts towards avoiding pain?

I put finger to keyboard precisely because I was becoming more and more aware of the commonality in my own stories and heartaches with those of others around me. I heard a great analogy once about how our own histories can offer others the rungs towards that place on the ladder where we are now. That our stories of that climb may give a platform of hope to others who are currently further down the rungs. Our individual life challenges are like giant, heavy metallic anchors that can sink us to the bottom of any deep cess pool. But our personal stories, when shared, can act as emergency life rafts for the sunken (or the sinking) to take refuge on and use to find their own way towards safer shores.

Of course, it is true that we benefit from and get the most impactful life lessons through our own actual experience rather than from hearing intellectual concepts about what that experience is like. There is no one-size-fits-all on this path: it is deeply personal, it is based on each person's own mind map, their likes, dislikes, fears and individual realm of belief and possibilities. So, I want you to think of this book not as a *how-to* book but rather a *from me to you* book. Please take from it what you need. It was written with one goal in mind and that was to remind others what I now know to be an absolute certainty: that we hold all the power for positive self-change in our lives, and no one or no thing can create that for us.

You are now, always have been and always will be enough.

Prologue

Knowing others is intelligence; knowing yourself is true wisdom.

– Lao Tzu –

Have you ever noticed that some of those itty-bitty songs our parents and grandparents sung us when we were itty-bitty babies are actually kinda grim? I mean, Jack and Jill's trip up that hill for what many would consider a basic human right, clean water, well, that didn't end well. And as for the right finger of the poor kid who was at first lucky enough to catch a fish alive. Ouchy. I got all the feels for the hopeful sailor who went out to sea in order to see the world. Nuthin' but the bottom of the deep blue sea sea sea for him. Every. Single. Time. And who doesn't have empathy for the sore heads of those cute little monkeys? C'mon. Those poor poppets were just trying to have some fun jumping on a bed. And all five of them went down.

But the one that really razzle dazzles me is the poor, fragile egg that sat, very innocently, high up, solving the world's problems on a wall. Doing what all kids imagine to be a really fun thing to do. What happens to him? He falls, doesn't he? Worse. He falls and then no one, not even *all* the king's horses and men, the entire battalion of the community's most powerful and trained army, could put him together again. And that's literally it. No more lyrics. It just ends, tragically, there. Now, tradition would have us believe that the more perfect and happy ending to that nursery rhyme might be the saving of that little source of animal protein by his fellow comrades. Sure, I have no doubt, even a vegan would crack a smile. But imagine just for a second if at the tender age of three (and beyond) we heard the story end with the words *with all of his might and a splash of some zen, Humpty put himself together again.* Now we're talkin'.

I can really feel for Humpty. There he was with this grand sense of perspective. High up on a wall. A rock-solid foundation underneath him, holding him up confidently. And then, BOOM. With absolutely no warning. The great fall. I mean, who, on this almighty planet, does not resonate with that feeling? The feeling that comes with a totally unexpected and enormously impactful fall from grace? And who wouldn't, lying cracked into a million tiny pieces on the floor, hope and pray for the saving grace of a royal army to make them better again? I have fallen off proverbial walls a million times over. And I have also relied on my dutiful army of people, wisdom and ideas to prop me back on up. Some of these rescues have felt momentarily healing and many provided me with immense feelings of gratitude.

There have been falls from walls that barely bruised my bottom on landing and many that required more serious triage or Band-Aids. But there was one particular fall that felt ironically dreamlike. Where the descent from the precipice felt inordinately long. From the life-threatening push to the crippling impact of concrete beneath me. Almost as if suspended in time. Or perhaps not actually really happening. But unlike these make-belief verses, this one was true.

Introduction

If it is to be, it is up to me
– William Johnsen –

Rare and deadly. Two words that altered my entire sense of personal stability. As my brand-spanking-new baby girl turned one year old, a doctor told me that there was a rather nasty head and neck cancer hiding in my face which fit that exact description. Rare. And deadly. The "C word" alone is enough to fill one's mind with horror-story futures. So, the two dramatic adjectives that got emphatically attached to my diagnosis did absolutely nothing to spare me from the mental catastrophes that quickly spewed forth into the crystal ball that I thought to be my mind.

Within seconds of hearing the crushing news, all my plans for a perfect family life that I had pinned my happiness on were immediately on the chopping board. My daughter's name played on a violent loop inside my head as the doctor casually spoke the words. Her name and the fast-forward visuals about all the milestones I would now not be there for were so loud to me that I stopped hearing what he was saying. How could the world be so cruel as to give me a rare and deadly head and neck cancer so soon after my beautiful daughter had arrived?

Until I was diagnosed, I had spent a large part of my life subconsciously assuming that I was invincible, taking risks and participating in life in a way that took for granted that bad things can happen. I guess that comes as much with youthful innocence as it does with adult arrogance, but let's all face into what we know undoubtedly to be true: invincibility could not be further from the truth as it relates to our physical bodies. They, whoever "they" are, are not pulling our legs when they say life is short and death is a certainty.

Sometimes, though, when something bad or unexpected happens to us, it is normal to feel a loss of control and empowerment, as if we are somehow just a victim of circumstance. There can be a yearning or a desperate feeling of just wanting to be saved. To be spared the crushing blow. Like everyone, I have lived a lifetime of feeling exposed to a myriad of circumstances, and surrounded by people, that offer up daily the potential for suffering and pain. And this has led to almost fifty years of trialling and experimenting with reliance on others to help me with the effort required to reduce that pain.

This diagnosis was a shocking and unwanted entry into my life that had me initially categorise it as an ending of some kind. However, looking back, I can see it now as a true beginning. The beginning of my journey towards finding an answer. An answer to the question I had been searching for all my life. When the chips are down, how is it that one should approach putting oneself back together again? Cancer coming into my life was the gateway. The catalyst, you could even call it, for me to discover the one with all the answers. *Youru.*

A *who-ru?* Well, that's a good bloody question. No, it is not a distinctive Australian way of saying "goodbye". It would be kind of foolish, don't you think, for me to start a book by saying Hooroo to you all. No, instead I am deliberately naming each one of you right up front, even before you might be ready to accept it for yourself, a Youru. Clearly, it is a made-up word. Clearly, it has no current formal meaning. But whilst totally fictional and not *yet* listed in the dictionary, it is my personal truth and my continual aspiration. And I would like to share with you how I personally define it and see if, together, we can somehow make it more commonly used vernacular.

I've done my research. A word gets into the dictionary when it is used by many people who all agree it means the same thing. You need to use it. First, you drop the word into conversation or writing. Check. Then others pick it up. Well, you are reading this book, so Check. Then its use starts to spread, an alert and wise dictionary editor may notice it has become part of mainstream life, et voilà, we have all become authors. To pass the muster, though, what you need is to satisfy three key criteria – frequent use, widespread use and meaningful use – before anyone will open the golden gates into the illustrious forever land of a dictionary.

Frequent use means it cannot be just a trendy flash in the pan that comes and goes; it needs to have staying power. Widespread use means an average adult is likely to encounter the word and know what it means. Meaningful use is not one I think we even need to explain or understand intellectually; it will hopefully be self-evident by the last page in this book. The bottom line is that this word does fill a really important gap not only in our language but also in our minds and our hearts, and I would like to move some part of the way, if not all of the way, towards filling that for myself and hopefully help you do the same if it resonates. It is not just intended by me as a clever, creative gimmick. But even if it never ends up in any universal glossary of words, that doesn't make it any less real.

If I did ever happen to come across a lexicographer in my life and had a chance to make a good pitch, here is where I would start:

The word **Guru** is defined in the Oxford English Dictionary as:

1. *a Hindu spiritual teacher.*
2. *an influential teacher or popular expert.*

In the Merriam-Webster Dictionary it is similarly defined:

1. *a personal religious teacher and spiritual guide in Hinduism.*
2. *a teacher and especially intellectual guide in matters of fundamental concern.*
3. *one who is an acknowledged leader or chief proponent.*
4. *a person with knowledge or expertise, an expert.*

Both of these sources of formal intelligence agree on a number of things. First, that when used in a spiritual context, there is a direct link to Hinduism. In Hinduism, the Guru is an ancient and central figure. A Guru is a teacher of skills, a counsellor, one who helps in the birth of mind and realisation of one's soul, who instils values and knowledge, an exemplar and an inspiration to others' personal growth. A Guru, as a shedder of light, does not even need to be a person but can be a teacher that comes to you in the form of an experience which itself has taught you in some way or has contributed to your personal evolution.

Hinduism is more than just one of the oldest religions in the world; it is a way of life, a body of wisdom available as a gift to us all. The major scriptures and philosophies of early classical Hinduism are contained in a life-affirming body of knowledge called the Vedas, which is where the word Guru emanated from. Guru is a Hindu word and is written in Sanskrit. Typically, words in Sanskrit are not translated by way of a defined literal meaning. Rather, they are interpreted as sounds or cognitions that are the expressions of a particular form. The word *Guru* is made up of two parts. *Gu* is an expression of darkness. And *ru* is an expression of remover. You get the picture. A Guru, by its technical definition, is a person or phenomenon who brings light and dispels darkness. Close your eyes and imagine that for just a second: *the. power. to. remove. darkness.* If I were a producer at Marvel, I know who my next superhero would be. And if I were a human being, which I think I am, I would certainly want to know how it was that I could possibly attain such a power.

Now watch me as I simply, yet with an immense sense of reverence and deep-seeded belief, replace *Gu* with *You*. *You-ru*. Don't get all technical on me now and say, hang on, are you saying I am the remover of myself? Not at all. Although, let's face it, we probably should all move ourselves out of the way as blockers of our own paths to happiness. What *Youru* means to me is that it is you, and only you, who can remove the darkness from your own life. I know I could just say that You are the Guru. But humour me, that would not be as fun or as empowering. And it would go against the other main idea opened up for exploration in this book, which is that there is no person, phenomena or experience beyond or outside of you that can bring the light to you eternally. It is, *spoiler alert*, already within you.

Let's go back for just a second to the English definitions and the common theme that a Guru is some form of expert or teacher. Sometimes it is because of this role that Gurus are typically also worshiped. But if the Guru is Youru, perhaps we can learn that the ultimate knower of all things is actually you and that it's time to start to worship yourself. Not in an arrogant, *I am the overseer of the entire kingdom of others, all of whom shall kneel before me*, power-hungry kind of a way. More in an *I don't need to live in exaltation of others or outsource the making of decisions as to whether I am happy* kind of a way. I am not saying that there is no place in our lives for Gurus outside of ourselves. There is a place for Gurus of all kinds, but they should be complimentary and not King.

I will share with you the stories of some of the people, things and ideas that I have given the reverential status of Guru in my life. That I have looked to in order to guide me towards where I wanted to be or save me from a particular adversity I have faced. I think almost everyone I know has at some point in time, and to varying degrees of success, knelt down before each type of Guru with the same goal in mind – salvation or answers. A Guru is by definition a teacher, right? So, it's not surprising that each one of them has left me with profound and unforgettable blessings and education, the way that all good Gurus should. Ultimately, though, none of these Gurus have brought me any kind of *lasting* fulfilment.

I don't think it's a stretch to say that, like many others, I have spent most of my life not in a state of having arrived but rather in a state of either constant searching or escaping. If we are not careful or more conscious, we may live our lives in a series of continual interchanging search and rescue missions.

A search mission means we are on the prowl to find or produce the perfect person, place or material thing that we are certain will bring us happiness or the answers to our unsolved questions. And don't get me wrong, we might, in fact, convince ourselves that we have found that, but experience has proven to me that it is always only temporary, as nothing is permanent in this relative world in which we live. It all has an ultimate end. Often when people are looking for hope in a trying situation, they say the words that *this too shall pass*. Which is true. But it is important to remember that all the good things or experiences in your life shall also ultimately pass. This is not said to be negative but rather to ponder the idea that living your life in sole reliance on a person, place or thing staying put forever is not a recipe for lasting fulfilment and is likely to cause you suffering at some point.

A rescue mission, on the other hand, finds you hatching an escape plan to remove the seemingly imperfect person, place or thing that, when you found it, didn't satisfy you after all. You start to run in another direction once the illusion of permanent fulfilment is washed away by the ever-changing external basket that you placed all your eggs in. And that can be scary, because it is then that you find yourself in the harrowing land of uncertainty. So, once that rescue mission is complete, guess what happens – fear of uncertainty or the incredibly uncomfortable unknown leads you back to the Search and Rescue hamster wheel.

There will always another mountain peak that is visible from the place where you settle after the search mission. But how would it feel to just be happy and fulfilled exactly where you are right now? It is possible with acceptance of what is. And it is possible if you do the work to move closer to the realisation that the only place you will find everlasting fulfilment is within you and that it is there already. Even if that seems like one of those clichéd, overly used phenomena that you cannot quite grasp or believe, for now just assume it is true. Or at least possible. And I will do my best to share with you how I came to trust it with certainty. There has gotta be a reason everyone keeps saying it, surely.

So let me now try, if I might, to give this new word *Youru* a meaning that we can aspire to have capture the attention of all lexicographers around the world. A new word in our vocabulary that allows us to name that which is already true: happiness can only be found within us and it is already there if we want, and if we know how, to access it. And even better than just a new name for ourselves, a new kind of reliable person to place at the altar every time we need a teacher or a guide. You. Let's give it a definition that becomes used every day, everywhere and which carries eternal meaning.

YOURU noun

(pronounced *you.ru*)

: a universal spiritual teacher.
// The *Youru* found personal enlightenment within and then from that place of inner baseline fulfilment took it to the greater world to share their wisdom.

: an influential teacher of oneself.
// A great *Youru* understands that the most lasting and evolutionary lessons and opportunities for change come from within and not outside of themselves.

: an expert who is popular with themself, first and foremost.
// The *Youru* doesn't seek the validation of other people or things "out there" for their own sense of self-love and from that place can love others unconditionally and with less dependence.

: an especially intellectual guide of oneself in all matters of fundamental concern.
// A *Youru* asks and relies on themself for the answer, understanding that they are the ultimate knower of all things and that it is already within them if they are conscious enough to be aware.

: one who acknowledges themself as the leader and chief proponent of their own life.
// The *Youru* refused to be a victim and give their power away to anyone or any circumstance in their outer environment or postpone their own enlightenment by waiting on it to come from the outer world.

It feels elusive, I get that. Where does one meet such a fine-sounding person? If *Youru* really is a word, if you can come to believe that the Guru to worship and look to for answers is, in fact, you, then liberation from some of the suffering is getting closer. I have heard enough wise people say that the extent to which you are convinced that it is others or external circumstances that are in charge of what you are experiencing is the exact extent to which you will suffer. As an interminable idealist, I would like to believe that all painful dependency on others or things outside of ourselves can be minimised and, one day, hopefully removed. That the freeing liberation from living at the mercy of an unstable and in-flux outer world can be experienced. A good Guru, one who truly knows that you, too, are Guru, would never take satisfaction in making you dependant on it. A true Guru would aspire to teach you greater self-sufficiency.

And if Youru is true-ru, then we are one step closer to a more conscious collective. One step closer to the cessation of all the individual importation businesses that endeavour to acquire happiness as if it were a commodity from *out there*, and instead the formation of individual exportation businesses that fill the marketplace with the self-love and inspiration capable of contributing to real and lasting evolutionary change. I want to be a part of that. I want to see that happen. Do-you?

PART ONE

Guru

CHAPTER ONE

Guru Parents

Grapes must be crushed to make wine. Diamonds form under pressure. Olives are pressed to release oil. Seeds grow in darkness. Whenever you feel crushed, under pressure, pressed, or in darkness, you're in a powerful place of transformation/transmutation. Trust in the process.

– Lalah Delia –

I wish I could say exactly what kind of family I was born into. But the truth is, I don't think anyone actually knows. How could I possibly know at age ground zero, or even by casting my mind back 40+ years, what the state of my family and everyone in it was at that moment in time? I also feel like any attempt to do so would be grossly tempered by how that family eventuated over the years to now, which is just plain bias.

But I can give you some facts. I was born in the year of 1976, and at that time my mother and father were still together and had already delivered my beloved big sister to the world. A couple of years after me came my other beautiful younger sister. And then there were three. We grew up in a small suburb called Strathfield, in New South Wales, Australia. My parents had both grown up there and both sets of my grandparents lived within streets of us and each other, so it was an easy walk to either set of Nan and Pop. All of our closest family friends were from the same area, we loved and knew our neighbours intimately and everyone went to the same schools as their parents did. The tribal village vibe was real.

I can still remember the precise phone number of our old

rotary dial telephone. My parents had renovated the original bungalow and added a second-floor extension, where my two sisters and I slept. Our three bedrooms were side by side, accessed from a communal landing out the front leading also to our own shared bathroom. I have vivid clarity about how each of our rooms was styled – totally representative of our individual personalities, with about the only commonality between them all being our collections of Cabbage Patch dolls. I can still see the poster that people met the minute they walked into my room which said "This is my room, like it or lump it" accompanied by visual images of an extremely messy and eccentric-looking room. Rebel much?

My sisters and I had a toy box on that landing full of dress-up and role- playing paraphernalia. We would often set up shops at our bedroom doors, and we would each go to visit the others' businesses, paying for their goods or services with Monopoly money. I recall that I always liked running a fortune-telling business. Outside of our comfortable four walls, I remember the route to the corner shop. I remember the annual trips to Terrigal Beach on the central coast of New South Wales and sliding on cardboard boxes down the steep infamous Skillion hill. And I remember Bobbie the Clown, who my mum used to hire for all of our birthday parties.

My everyday memories from that period paint a young life almost formulaic in its uncomplication. I guess you could describe it as simple suburbia. It was nice. It was happy. I was so well looked after and provided for. Many would say incredibly privileged, and I would not disagree. And everyone else seemed pretty happy too. I went to the local Catholic school, and I am told I was quite enthusiastic, empathetic and reasonably bright even if a tad melodramatic, opinionated and annoying too.

The Organisation for Economic Co-operation and Development has suggested that the most formative years for young children are between the ages of one and eight, and it is during this period that a child's newly developing brain is most plastic and responsive to change as neural circuitry is formed and established as a result of a combination of genes, environment and experience. Any unsafe or negative experiences or interactions during this time can have tremendous impact which can affect a child's potential in the later years of their life.

It is indisputable that a young child's home environment can play a key role in influencing their chances for optimal personal development. I know of nothing in my first eight years that could have possibly contributed to anything seriously limiting to my potential. Quite the opposite, in fact. I was safely housed, I was nutritionally fed, I was incredibly well educated and I was deeply loved by my mum, dad, two sisters and everyone in the community around me. It would be remiss of me not to credit up front these foundational years of my early life for contributing to my resilience for coping with what came next.

Separation anxiety

It is critically important for me to emphasise at this point that one of my fundamental beliefs in life is that all points of view are relative to the owner. Any story that I tell is just a story as seen and experienced from my own eyes and heart.

I am absolutely certain that, seen from someone else's vantage point, there might be facts I have left out, facts I have misinterpreted, facts I have failed to see or take into account. But I am OK with that because this is just my story. This account of what happened is purely how I saw or experienced it at such a young and impressionable age.

At worst I was exposed to some sense of a lack of marital bliss between my parents. Maybe some badly concealed fights. Perhaps even some mild feelings of loathing between them. I have a strong memory of tiptoeing halfway down the stairs that led from our bedrooms to spy on the shenanigans happening on the ground floor. There was a precise step from which you could see directly into the family room and open kitchen. I would poke my head through the timber poles to get an even better angle. My memory has me getting my head stuck, so serious were my efforts to see further or hear more about what was going on between my parents. Their fighting had increased, and it became more and more clear to all of us that Mum and Dad were just not getting along.

I think as you enter the final two years of primary school, around age eight to ten, your perceptual capabilities and interpretive skills become much stronger. Not that the cues were incredibly subtle, mind you. High-heeled shoes were thrown wildly. Doors were slammed shut. Dinners were refused to be made. Eyes were perpetually rolled. Physical berths got wider. Whilst of course our parents did their best to shield us from the worst of it, the often invisible but tangible tension was thick enough for us to draw our own silent conclusions.

Quite often you hear stories of parents making decisions to stay together for the sake of the children. Thankfully, my parents did not succumb to that mythology. Nothing good would have come of that for any of us. They separated when I was nine years old. The emotional upheaval this caused was more than any of us would have wished for or expected. But it also led to more growth, opportunities and personal evolution for myself but also for my best friend, my mum. Eventually.

I can still remember the precise moment – the space I occupied, perched on the outer arm of our family room sofa, crouched around my mum, her best friend and my sisters – when breaking news interrupted an otherwise ordinary day. Dad had left the building. It was also from this very same second that my mother commenced what has been a lifelong concerted effort not to disparage our father or seek to diminish him in our eyes. Irrespective of the hurt we were to learn she had experienced as a result of his life choices, I am grateful to this day for her commitment not to try and tarnish her children's sense of security that comes from their relationship with their own father.

My mother was and remains full of life. All of my early memories of her are of someone who was stunningly beautiful, the life of the party, the centre of attention (and loved it). A mother who filled us with confidence about who we were and what we could achieve. She was inordinately kind and generous to us kids and to everyone around her. But also someone who was silly, loved a good goss and didn't take herself too seriously. Most of all she was hugely enthusiastic, about everything. And when I say everything, I leave not a single particle of life out of that equation. Her passion and enthusiasm was, and still is, all-consuming. I am pretty certain I could sue Energizer Batteries for misleading and deceptive conduct for claiming that the Energizer Bunny has the most continuous, indefinite and lasting energy. Nuh-uh. That would be my mum. She could run rings around that cool little drum-beating rabbit.

It would not be useful, or even accurate, for me to retrospectively analyse or even seek to find out what the micro-causes that led to my parents' marriage breaking down might have been, because I am sure they would both fairly accept their own individual contributions to that outcome. But there was a definite and clear deciding stroke in this fifteen-year-long match. An unexpected backhand shot that sliced what was one, into two. An extramarital affair.

I was so ridiculously close to my mum. More than that, I was eerily similar to her in my nature. I do not think, therefore, I will ever be able to adequately explain why, then, I made the decision after their separation to leave my mum and two sisters and move in with my dad. But let me give it my best stab.

It was not an instant decision. And I know it sent seismographic shockwaves of disbelief through my family when I did make it, especially for Mum. I was a super sensitive child. I was a people pleaser. I liked being liked. I felt bad when I saw someone sad or suffering. I could not even watch the TV show *Lassie* out of anticipatory fear for the life perils of those that the divine infamous collie would rescue. I recall, even as early as primary school, that I was always the kid who would flock to the most wounded bird when it came to making friends. Making a beeline towards the person who looked the most alone or in need. And in many ways, I think that is what I did with Dad. No one else was going with him, and we all loved him so much, so I guess I thought *someone ought to*.

There were, however, other influences. After the initial separation, my sisters and I spent the next year or so hopping between life with Mum and life with Dad – overnight we had acquired not just a step-parent but also step-siblings. As the weeks and months went by, I became inextricably intertwined with this second family set-up. So much so that at the pretty tender age of eleven I banished myself entirely from the life of my mother and two sisters to live full time with my dad and his new family. I am talking complete and total separation. I did not see any of them for six long years. Ouch.

There was an extremely ugly and volatile period after I made this monumental decision. I have learnt from this time in my life how easily influenced the hearts and minds of young children are amidst a family breakdown. Divorce can be an exceedingly difficult arena for children to navigate. Separation, it would seem, is not a term reserved only for the parents.

Hello, is it me you're looking for?

My mother made many unspeakably painful efforts to see me. She would come to try to get me from my school, from my paternal grandparents' when I was there, or even just on weekend visits in the early days before I chose not to go back. Each and every time I rejected her, which I do recall being immeasurably hard for both of us. And over time, as I got older and more engrained in this new "other family" life, it became the norm that I just didn't spend time with my mum and two sisters anymore.

We lived completely separate lives, and we were not aware of what the other was doing. It was not until our reunion that I fully understood the severity and significance of this kind of disconnection. One of the most positive and pivotal moments in both my own and my older sister's life was the day we were reunited.

She had gotten through high school, and I was just coming up to the finish line. In the latter years of my high school journey,

I had become extremely dissatisfied with my living arrangements. "Home" felt unpredictable and unsettling, like living on eggshells that could crack at any moment. I would use the Art Gallery and the State Library of New South Wales as two little caverns of quiet and calm and as the places where I did all my studying for the higher school certificate. I was quite literally always at one or the other.

One day I was sitting at the same long communal table by the state library window that I always sat at, and as I looked up from my copious research and notes, I caught a glimpse of who I was certain was my older sister, Kate. I did a double take. Not because I was unsure it was her but because it had been so damn long. In honesty, I did hesitate for a second. I even think I panicked a little. I was not sure after all this time how I would be received, and I was also just such an anxious person at this stage in my life that I didn't know what to do or say and so I froze for a nanosecond.

I knew deep down in my heart that I had to get up, and as the anxiety passed, the excitement started to brew. I walked over to my sister with just the faint remains of trepidation. We had been estranged for so long that when I tapped her on the shoulder and said "Kate?" she was momentarily unable to even recognise me. We laugh about it now, but she actually had to ask me who I was! The penny obviously dropped a few seconds into the conversation, but imagine that for just a second, not recognising your own sister. Without a lot more conversation, my sister led me immediately out into the corridor of the library entrance towards the old coin payphones and dialled our mother's number.

Until I was an adult, I was oblivious to the pain and suffering that my mum and sisters had all endured because of my decision to live with my dad. Equally, though, they were unwittingly blind to what my experience came to be. The term *sliding door moment* does not even remotely do justice to this choice that I made to go live with my dad. That term became popularised as meaning "seemingly inconsequential moments that nonetheless alter the trajectory of future events". It is undeniably true that this particular decision is the one that has had the most gravitas in terms of having altered my life's trajectory. However, there was nothing inconsequential about not seeing my mum and sisters for such a long and pivotal period of my life and personal development. It was enormously significant. Like, ginormously enormously significant.

The U-turn

There are so many words to describe the feelings associated with such a grand and important U-turn back towards my mum and sisters. First there is the heaviest of heavy guilt and trepidation. *Will they even want to see me? Will they still love me? Will I fit in?* Then there is the anticipatory elation at the thought of seeing them again. An almost wild curiosity. *What have they been doing all this time? What are they like now? What might we start to do together?*

The road was rocky at first. I showed up with intense emotional baggage and, of course, they still had their own pain backpacks on too. I was so sensitive, so hyper-dramatic, so needy and massively fearful of rejection. Naturally, my sisters had an incredibly close bond and lots of in-jokes that I was "out" of. Led entirely by my own insecure mind, and not through any of their actions, there were moments when I felt like I might never be part of a happy family again.

But over the next few years, we all shared in our own ways what the experience and separation from one another had meant for each of us. Some of it incredibly hard to hear and share, but we did it slowly, respectfully and in our own unique and individual ways. To all of our credit, with persistence and open hearts, we have rebuilt incredibly close and bonded relationships. We are all good friends and a loyal, united family of four proud and happy women.

Human beings have a natural tendency to hang their happiness hat on the existence of others in their lives. Like parents. Like family. It is normal to grow up believing that a perfect nuclear family will bring you great joy and personal success. Or be there to remove darkness for you when the life lights dim for a moment. But like all the altars of "others" that you bow to in order to find fulfilment or salvation, there will undoubtably be some curses.

Having said that, for every peril, there is a promise. For every storm, there is a sunset. From almost all salutations to the altars of Gurus come offerings. Blessings that you cannot forget to be thankful for. I try when I can to take whatever learnings that feed my soul and serve my life positively into the next phase and then leave the rest behind.

The timeless teachings of Jude-ism

Over the years I have joked about starting my own religion. The religion of *Jude-ism*. The teachings of which have stood the test of time and remain relevant in my life to this day. I call my mum playfully by a shortened version of her name, Judes. She has a unique and identifiable character that is very easy to take the mickey out of. My sisters and I have a lot of fun paying her out about some of her more amplified personality features. And it's her fault. She gives us such good fodder.

Judes is prone to a bit of exaggeration, a trait I seem to have inherited from her for sure. She can add a bit of dramatic flair to any situation. If one of us calls her and explains that we are a *tiny* bit stressed, Mum will relay it to another one of us as having heard that we are feeling *TOTALLY DISTRESSED*. Her biggest fear in life is not whether she will die but rather whether she will find a car park. She even has a prayer she says (out loud) as she approaches all events in her car, *"Hail Mary, full of grace, please find me a parking space"*, which my own daughter now uses from the back seat with an equally theatrical panic. She's such good fun.

But through her own rise from the ashes and emergence as a strong and successful woman, she has imprinted upon me a can-do mindset in the face of challenge. She is known for reminding all of us to have an attitude of gratitude for what we have rather than a focus on what we are lacking. An outlook that encourages giving back to those who need it most. She has taught me to see life not as a glass that is just half full but rather one that is bountiful and overflowing.

Judes had two sayings that she used often to motivate us, which I still carry with me everywhere I go. Both of them borrowed by her from the great Henry Ford. Whenever any of us were stuck in a moment of self-doubt about our capability to do or achieve something, or catastrophising about a moment that had not yet manifested, she would remind us, in her impassioned tones, "Whether you think you can or you think you can't – you are right." It was a very early lesson and represents the planting of the first seed of my own growing belief in the immense power of my mind.

If she could see I was ever stuck in a habitual, stagnating pattern and blaming the world out there for why I could not progress, she would again echo Mr Fords words: "If you always do what you've always done, you'll always get what you've always got." These very words could whip me out of the ever-repeating known into a world of entirely new actions and hence outcomes. Even the simple act of walking a different path each day to the same destination can be demonstrative of the spirit of this guidance, which really is to change your perspective if you are looking for an alternative view. To try something different if you want a different result.

These pearlers have carried me through periods of inertia, lack of motivation and lingering self-doubt. However, the absolute diamond in my own rougher period as a young adult came from my mum gifting me with the book *Creative Visualization* by Shakti Gawain. A book about using the power of your imagination to create what you want in your life – to manifest your deepest desires. I actually think that book was the very first foray I had into the world of personal development and awareness. And it was a foray that has literally never stopped since.

In many respects I can look back and proudly state that I have proactively self-taught myself towards greater wholeness. My passion (read: obsession) for personal evolution and development started early and remains strong. In fact, I have read only one or two fictional books in my entire life. I don't even like make-believe movies that much and have a distinct preference for true stories and documentaries – anything that can fill me with more knowledge about how to find a solution to emotional or life problems.

At this particular stage of my life, though, as I left high school and started university, I was looking more for the magic pills, instantaneous fairy dust or prescriptive guides on precisely how to get happy, how to remove pain, how to get what it was that I *thought* I wanted. So, at that time, I used the visualisation techniques offered in her book in a more surface-level way than I do now. I scoured books like Shakti's for the quick fixes, the *how-tos*, and ignored (or perhaps just didn't academically comprehend at the time) the foundational and spiritual underlying knowledge and wisdom, the *whys*. That came later.

Regardless, I certainly took from it what I needed at the time. I learned that if you wanted to manifest something in your life, you had to imagine that you had it right now. There was no power in imagining yourself having it at some point in the future. Or guess what? You would always be in a position where it was coming soon, rather than it being here right now. No, you had to faithfully presume, see it in your mind's eye, your heart and soul, that what you wanted was already here and then creatively imagine it into existence.

It was a sophisticated explanation of the more marketing-savvy approach taken by an infamous book that took the world by storm, *The Secret* by Rhonda Byrne. Once I'd popped into the whole power-of-manifestation bubble, I gobbled up *The Secret* like a hungry beggar. Again, the offer on a silver platter, to understand the laws of nature that govern all of our lives that enable us to self-create, with our own simple intention, a joyful life. It seems as if my desire for self-sufficiency was there in my subconscious from the very beginning of my life journey, but over time, with more knowledge and life experience, what that meant and how to attain it matured and clarified.

I actually think a lot of sceptics (including my friends as

I would try to shove it down their throats as if it were a three-Michelin-star spiritual meal) wrote this book off as being a far-fetched maniacal promise that offered people unrealistic expectations about what they could get from the world. The theory was similar to Shakti's, which was that first you had to ask the Universe for what you wanted, then you had to believe with your whole heart that what you desired (and which was unseen) was already here. And then you had to feel how you would feel once it arrived. They coined this the *Law of Attraction*.

The basic premise and process is to "Ask, Believe, Receive", which, of course, sounds very uncomplicated and enticingly easy. Too easy, the non-believers would say. Perhaps the documentary film version of the book did not do itself any justice when they had adults massaging their temples whilst staring into store windows at unaffordable diamonds, or kids imagining themselves with bikes as cool as their mate's next door, all of which was then almost instantaneously delivered to the aspirant. But if you can look past the exaggeration into the more basic underlying premise, the gold is there.

Whether or not it was the perfect communication of the spiritual ideal, I do actually believe the basic tenet of it and have used it successfully on multiple occasions. I consider myself a powerful manifester. I kept it more on the down-low back then for fear of looking like a whack job. Whenever it has not been successful, I can admit openly that it was likely due to either my lack of a true understanding and belief about why it was possible or, perhaps, the absence of the requisite authentic intention and blind faith. I have also come to learn that sometimes what we *want* is not always what we *need* and that we must make allowances for that.

I was nowhere near ready in these earlier days of my life to try to imagine and believe being happy, secure and conscious. Being a victim was just easier and somehow seemed more comfortable (so I thought). But I was very happy to experiment with the concept of the Law of Attraction, and so I started to use it for more concrete things, for example manifesting a job I really wanted to get. I would do really kooky things. Like after an interview, I would get in the car and pretend that my phone rang, answer it with nobody really on the receiving end and then engage in a faux conversation with the interviewer who was calling me to tell me I had the job.

I would literally have the conversation out loud, including pauses for when the other person "spoke". *"Are you serious? I have the job? That is amazing! Oh my goodness, that salary is almost double what I asked for. You are so kind. When do I start?"* Did I ever do this with a real-life human passenger in the car seat next to me? Well, no. But I make no apologies because these superpowers, these Jude-isms that my mum ignited in me after such a sad phase in our relationship, have been, and remain, an inordinate blessing in my life.

Everything that is happening is evolutionary

*I had to make you uncomfortable
otherwise you never would've moved.*

– The Universe –

I mentioned earlier in this chapter that from the pain came evolution, eventually, and I wasn't lying. As much as it is hard to admit, consciousness and growth aren't achieved at anywhere near the magnitude after a happy event as they are after a so-called sad one. Wouldn't it be nice, though, if people could find a way towards consciousness and growth without the need of a kick-ass trauma? But that is the super-saver in me talking. Let's face it, Nietzsche hit the mark when he said that what does not kill us will make us stronger. But I would probably take that one step further and say, this is true, but only if you can adjust your visual and mental acuity sharply enough to see the gift in the trauma that is almost invariably hiding amongst the bushy thorns.

My own sense of perception started very, very, very narrowly, let me tell you. I could not have sensed even the most glaring of bright lights in the dark when I was younger and could wallow in my self-pity with an unhealthy level of gusto. With time I have come to learn that it is far more beneficial to relish in my painful childhood experience as having forced me into greater personal evolution than to give attention to the woe-is-me feeling that arises more naturally. Sometimes immediately after I experience trauma, the thorns often feel just far too prickly to reach in and pull out the gift. But I would still try as hard as I could, with the passage of time and distance from the event, to start to draw on my inner Steve Jobs.

In a famous speech he delivered to college graduates in the early 2000s, Jobs encouraged the captivated audience with his wise advice that even if we cannot understand our challenges in the moment, to just trust that the dots will somehow connect one day when we are looking backwards. Without any evidence, and perhaps propped up by some of that resilience I was lucky enough to develop in my early years, I do believe that there is always a reason why something is happening, good or bad. And that if we are open to it, we might just come to see that it was for progressive or necessary change in our lives.

A very wise man in my life once used a particularly powerful visual analogy to share his view not just on the reality of how life plays out with all its ups and downs but also why that is a good thing. He shared with me the image of a heart monitor, an ECG reading that records the rhythm and beat of the heart, the central governor of a thriving physiology, the ultimate source of and enabler to experience life's purpose, which is to love.

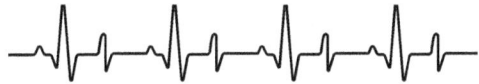

He used this image to help me understand that life is in the living and that all it has to offer your ability to evolve can be found in both the highs and the lows. In both the elevated peaks of apparent or momentary triumph and in the devastating troughs of tragedy or challenge. And just like in a healthy ECG, these peaks and troughs are actually an indicator that you are alive, that you are breathing, that you are still here and capable of participating. All too often, we make a false assumption that the rollercoaster ride of good times and not-so-good times that we all find ourselves unwittingly on is somehow unfair, is not a life well lived, is a sign of turmoil and ultimate dissatisfaction. But think for a moment of the alternative in this analogy. What if your heart monitor looked more like this?

In scientific terms, that would categorically, unequivocally and in no uncertain terms mean that you were, in fact, dead. Tell me, how can growth ever come from that? How can the seemingly invisible opportunities cleverly disguised as impossible situations ever make their way into our stories then?

How, if we are dead, can we move to a time in our lives where our awareness is expansive enough to make those gifts that are delivered through pain less invisible and more glaringly obvious? I found this analogy to be pretty compelling. A really helpful platform from which to accept with less disappointment and more grace the unavoidable fact that life is not always a smooth ride. A motivator to stop aspiring for monotonous flatlines and rather focus my attention on how to cope with, adapt to and learn from both the rough waves and the mountaintops.

You will have all heard of the psychological condition that onsets after the experience of significant trauma, post-traumatic stress disorder, more commonly known as PTSD. I wonder, though, how many of you have heard about an equally valid but less commonly known outcome of trauma: which is post-traumatic growth. One of the best books on this phenomenon that I have read is by Jim Rendon, titled *Upside: The New Science of Post-Traumatic Growth*.

The author convincingly reports on this emerging field of psychological research that shows how the suffering caused by traumatic events can be harnessed as a force for self-improvement and success rather than destruction. His words sung to me with the intense power of the Harlem Gospel Choir. It made a lot of sense to me that I could, if I wanted to, choose to think about my experience as a young child separated from my mum and sisters as a pivot point that may have turned me towards things of much more significance and importance, or led me in new directions that may never have been appealing had I not experienced that pain at all.

Would the Awesome Foursome of me, my mum and sisters, and all the juicy goodness that flows from it, have been formed with such enthusiasm and lasting nourishment had we not been through this upheaval together? Would I have become the independent, capable woman that I am had I not had to move out of home at a relatively young age and learn the value of earning money and hard work? Would I have volunteered for community organisations all my life to help others if I had not experienced my own suffering? Hell, would I have even discovered Youru if this first part of my life had not led me onto the next one and the one after that? Perhaps all of this growth was exactly what was meant to transpire from the trauma.

I remember someone telling me once to think of life's challenges like the tension in a tightly stretched guitar string and then quickly turn my mind to the magical music that always comes from it. How beautiful is that sentiment? It affords me the option of reinterpreting the reason for trauma from meaningless pain to purposeful progression. It enables me to connect the dots that once were just random markings on my life path and start to make sense of some of the prior darkness.

The events themselves can never be altered, the hard facts will always remain the same, but the meaning you give the memories of those experiences can become more inspired. Maybe, just maybe, challenges in our lives are normal and to be expected. And release from suffering can come when such challenges cease to make us so unhappy. There is a beautiful ancient Sufi saying that "when the heart weeps for what it has lost, the spirit rejoices for what it has found", and that is just the way I like to try now to look back at past trauma.

The utility of forgiveness

Have you ever had the realisation while you are busy hating on someone for something they have allegedly done to you that you are the one getting drenched from the toxic anger storm and they seem to be gliding gleefully through the snow without a care in the world? And then seeing that only causes the internal shit storm to get even more wild and intolerable? This learning about the utility of forgiveness is so simple to understand but so goddamn hard to do. It has taken me literally years and countless failed attempts.

Once you are in this tornado of anger towards another, the very feeling that you are wanting your enemy to feel is now being felt by you and, worse than that, all self-imposed. How much worse does it feel when, after that happens, you can see your enemy jumping around as happy as Peppa Pig in muddy puddles, relishing in the impact your own anger for them has had on you? At this point, don't even bother with an umbrella because you are well and truly soaked in your own hatred downpour. This fruitless cycle is perfectly explained by the adage that anger is like swallowing poison and expecting the other person to die. Even just writing that makes me feel so stupid for the years' worth of anger pills I swallowed after I first left my father's home.

There is a beautiful Zen Buddhist story about two monks who came across a woman struggling to cross a river, asking for help. The senior monk picked her up, carried her across safely and then continued on his journey. Struck by their vow not to touch a woman, the other monk asked him why he did such a thing, and the older monk replied, "Brother, I set her down on the other side of the river, why are you still carrying her?" It is true that carrying around old hurts really only hurts ourselves, and ruminating on them only weighs us down further. All my fortressed anger ever did was ruin perfectly good experiences and relationships that were to come into my life. Looking back, I wish I had cut some of my adolescent anger short through forgiveness way earlier than I did.

Rightly or wrongly, I left my father's home with anger about what had happened and about my own tumultuous experience in living with him and his new family. It often felt that his new family was always the focus and the priority, leading to feelings of abandonment over the years. Some of that anger was outwardly expressed but also loads of it internally repressed. It was definitely the kind of anger that negatively impacted how I related to him but also to others in my life.

I distinctly remember the moment I decided to start to move towards giving forgiveness to my dad for some of my anger towards him. It had become abundantly clear that I needed to release the negative feelings I had about my childhood experience for my own health and wellbeing.

I can honestly, hand on heart, say that while I don't choose anymore to spend all my days with Dad and his new family, I hold no more conscious grudges. There may be a few whisperings of pain and resentment lingering in the hallways of my past, but if I really got called to do so, I think I could quieten them even more. That's progress, trust me. On refection, there are days when I have asked myself whether it was Dad I needed to forgive or, in fact, myself. I am still working on that one.

I find extreme solace in remembering that our parents did the best they damn well could based on what they themselves knew or had experienced in their own lives. At the very least we owe our very existence to them. I try at a minimum to have gratitude for the body that they are responsible for creating, in an effort to maintain a sense of unity amongst moments of tension. Fact of the matter is, these days I would rather be well than be the winner of the argument about who really was to blame. It's that simple. Even if, to justify our position, we tell ourselves its harder or more complicated than that.

We are all born into some kind of family. And if you are lucky enough to get consistently reliable comfort and refuge from that nest then, by all means, lay those delicious and healthy life eggs. But you see it everywhere. Cruel separation of families or seemingly unwarranted or hurtful abandonment by family members can also come. And so total reliance on parental love cannot be your only source of steadiness. Let's face it, even if you are in a family nest fit for an Eagle King, the kindest of birds still have beaks that bite and claws that scratch. Even in a good and stable family, attaching your sense of self-worth and happiness to their validation or love for you is risky because it, too, can change with people's moods, opinions and life experiences.

CHAPTER TWO

Guru Partner

*How people treat you is their karma;
how you react is yours.*

– Wayne Dyer –

Whenever I think about any kind of sole reliance on a lover or a partner for my happiness, disturbing images of Tom Cruise sliding enthusiastically across my mind's eye in just his pink shirt, white socks and banging out a tune into his candlestick microphone appear. It is just plain risky business is what it is. Anyone who is anyone, who is anyone who has been through a break-up is going to back me up here. I know there are some rare specimens in the Love Jungle who have been in the same loving relationship since they first locked horns. But when you ask some of them what they would do if the other left them? Well, they would die. Now, I may not be an expert naturist, but I am pretty sure David Attenborough would agree that extinction should not be the evolutionary outcome of a relationship bust-up. But it is how we often feel and for some fairly valid reasons.

Missile levels of information are ricocheting towards us from all directions from the second we are born and are loaded from so many different weapons – the opinion of others, family, media, advertisers, movie makers – that there is a perfect someone "out there" who is going to deliver us *unending* happiness. And with that conveyance will come an exemption from any kind of fluctuation in life. Putting aside the dangerous fact that this merciless shooting ignores that permanence is a lie and that change is a certainty, such a divine and enticing promise naturally leads to a serious sense of rigid attachment. If I find that perfect someone and then I let them go, or they are cruelly removed from my life, then it is not just the relationship that is over but also my own personal serenity.

The more painful bullet, though, is the one that carries the message that if one doesn't find such a demi-god at all, their life will be somehow less complete. This burning shot has catapulted me into intensely long and wasteful periods of postponing any joy at all in my life while waiting for this supposed Supreme Being to appear. Equally long periods squandered longing for the day (that never actually came) when a certain one I had found and given away my own power to would give it back in the form of total love and adoration for me.

There are, of course, tiny grains of truth amongst the shrapnel. It is undeniably true that our partners can bring us moments of incredible satisfaction and happiness and fulfil our lives in ways that might not have been possible without their presence. But it misses the bullseye of absolute truth, which is that, at any juncture, this other person could leave or become dissatisfied with us. And if we do not have enough self-love to fill the gaping wound, if our self-identity is so tightly wrapped up in their love for us rather than our own love for ourselves, then we just might be in trouble.

Nobody needs neediness

Stop trying to be liked by everybody.
You don't even like everybody.

– Unknown –

This all may make me sound like an embittered old bird who has had too many of her pretty feathers plucked out by cantankerous old crows. But it is not true. I am a love loyalist. I am a romantic novel living a human experience. You will not find me at a "Freedom from Relationships" rally waving a placard that insists on total independence, at liberty from all loving experiences with others. But I would happily join resistance efforts to any movement that sought to shackle my sense of self-satisfaction to someone else. I am not aspiring for emancipation from love, only its powerful stronghold on my own self-reliance.

I have now found a deeply satisfying love with my husband that, yes, the goal of which is to stay together until one of us passes rather than leaves by free will. The trouble is that he doesn't find neediness sexy in any way. And thank god for that. But also, a little bit what you talkin' about, Willis? Cause I *do* need him. Taking inspiration, though, from his attraction to independence and his own bedazzling self-surety, I have started to traffic my non-neediness efforts into a faster-moving thoroughfare. My husband would call it, at best, a casual stroll, but based on my past experience with trying to make headway through a relationship traffic jam whilst driving at a super needy pace, trust me, my momentum is picking up.

This movement has been fuelled mostly by one epic break-up that I now take a lot more personal responsibility for than I did at the time. Also, by the irritation that I have at myself for having depended for so long on the love of someone else for my own happiness. It was as if I had put all my personal self-worth on extended lay-by when I should have just paid for it up front, brought it home and experienced the fruits of my purchase a lot earlier than my then-deficient mindset pay cheque allowed.

There is not a single person who lived by my side during the period of this particular break-up (correction: repeated series of break-ups) that would express any inkling of positive sentiment about wanting to see me go through it. Or, more so, about wanting to accompany me along the arduous journey towards dissolution, ever again. And I mean nobody. Why on earth would they? It was a real-life shit-show. Such a brutal oscillation between the bliss of togetherness, the happy highs, and the deep burrows of break-ups, the burdensome lows. Jake and I went up and back down again with more velocity than the gravitational pull of humans to Earth's centre. We had more ups and downs than the most epic of all rollercoaster rides. During the entire course of the relationship, which traversed on and off for about seven of my journeys around the Sun, it was woe is me and so woe must be everyone else. Whenever he left me, it was woe is him and so woe must everyone else think of him too. Tragic, really, now that I look back on it.

I met Jake through a mutual friend. It was at a wedding that we both attended where the initial earlier introduction became more of a pursuit. It was really clear at this event that Jake and I had good banter. He intrigued me, a lot. His look was classic handsome rugby player. The man very clearly pumped some iron. It gave him an uber masculine vibe which felt reassuringly comforting to me. Almost bodyguard protector-like in his physique. One would look at him and assume he would ooze confidence (or arrogance), but almost immediately from our chats I sensed a vulnerability, an underlying cynicism or almost bitterness about life. He was a deeply loving teddy bear inside his Terminator body. It was intuitively clear to me that he was someone completely unaware of his brilliance.

His darker edge came out in his humour, though, which

was a huge connection point for us. We shared the silliest obsession with *Little Britain* and any jokes relating to poo. We would sit for what felt like hours giggling like children at each other's stupid jokes or random comments and observations about the world around us. The connection was clearly on an intellectual level and our chats became longer and deeper and some might say even ventured into the bizarre, but we truly understood each other. It was like we developed our very own language.

In the lead up to meeting Jake (and perhaps even more so after he left), it was wildly apparent that a younger, happier Single Sarah was starting to retreat further and further backstage to make way for the new star of the show about to proudly make her entrance, Desperate Debbie. Many can relate to this archetypal character. Her stage name is known only by those who talk about her behind her back. To her, she is just Debbie. Ain't nuthin' desperate about her. No way. She is a lean, mean, come-get-me machine, convinced that she is the one fish that John West should never reject. She tells herself that she doesn't need a man to bring her satisfaction, yet she goes to bed bawling after watching *Love Actually* or after having been out all night with all of her married friends. She cocks her head and says "Awwwwwwwwwwww" in an itty-bitty baby voice whenever her friends coo over pictures of their newborns doing relatively basic things but later that day un-friends that annoying, over-the-top Stage Mum from Facebook. Desperate Debbie spends most of her sweet days trying to work out why, as an accomplished, attractive woman, nobody wants her.

Denial Debbie is also always lurking sheepishly in the wings. And when that stage light finally illuminates her, the impact can be heartbreaking. The fruitlessness of hiding from the fact that your happiness is precariously hinged on the attainment of "the one" gets harder to continue denying. You *know*, even if you can't yet say it out loud, that marriage and a baby carriage is all that will allow you to feel like you have arrived. And then the pursuit of it becomes nothing other than excruciating to watch and to experience. Desperation has a pungent, repulsive aroma to anyone entering the wearer's zone of thirsty longing. It is a smelly signal to the other that the expectation upon them is going to be high, which can be scary.

When I met Jake, it would have smelled as if I had bathed in this nauseating fragrance for over a year and never washed it off. But somehow he managed to wade through it, and we found each other. Don't get me wrong, he and I had so many genuine and good reasons for having been magnetised towards each other. Our lust for deep and challenging conversations and topics, and a deep admiration for what each other had traversed in life to date made our bond feel tight (and often right). However, I can see now how my pursuit of Jake was also an unfair, unsolicited extension of the unfulfilled yearning that I had for my dad to choose me and to be there for me. In many ways I was expecting Jake to fill the role of a replacement paternal protector.

Jake was probably more capable of smoothly sailing towards me through the neediness ocean because he was approaching me in his own get-away boat, on a mission to break free of his own past issues associated with parental love. Coming at each other and trying to form a lasting love without individual baseline happiness and satisfaction with ourselves as we were, on our own and without the salvation of the other, was, in the glorious light of hindsight, a trite exercise.

Both of us, probably relatively unconsciously, sought from each other, rather than from ourselves, the validation that we had missed from caregivers. Neither expectation was fair. With the very best of intentions, we set ourselves up for failure before we began to try. Despite enormous efforts on both our sides, I personally felt totally incapable of meeting his needs, and I am pretty sure he felt the same way about mine. Looking back, it hardly feels like those revelations should have caused the need for any kind of mental surprise party. But both of us hung around like that one party goer who just can't bear to see the night end, reluctant to leave the soirée at a decent hour of the night.

I think it's important to recognise that the outsourcing of your self-assurance to your partner – depending on them to have confidence in your own abilities and character – has ripple effects beyond just you. I cannot count on all the people in the world's fingers and toes the number of times that I would have criticised Jake over the years for *his* failures to meet *my* needs rather than recognising that this was actually my responsibility and not his. If my partner is busy silently grappling with his own internal shit, the last thing he needs is me, the other mad hatter telling him that my suffering is a result of his failures or deficiencies. And vice versa. In this battlefield of neediness and co-dependency, you start to also immaturely hate any person who might see your relationship issues or break-ups from your (ex-)partner's point of view, and so friends are also regrettably lost in the foggy haze of the victim profile you have created for yourself.

These reflections are about growth and self-development, the blessings that I have taken from this dangerous deification of a partner to such godly status as being able to single-handedly remove darkness from my own past. That power always has and always will lie in my own hands, and it was not right for me to try to place it in someone else's.

Fact of the matter was, until we found individual self-love, we just could not do justice to the genuine love we also had for each other. And with neither of us yet in a state of life consciousness where we were fully cognisant of what we were doing, we were a tad useless for each other, and the blame game led to multiple life-crashing break-ups, followed intermittently by hallowed reunions, but ultimately ending in not-so-happily ever after. When we broke up for the final time, Jake said some poignant words to me that in the moment made me want to slap him in the face but that now make perfect sense. As I shamelessly begged him one more time to please stay, he said that one day I was going to look back and thank him for this because he genuinely believed that us breaking up would be the right thing for me. What felt like a poor excuse for another poor decision to leave me, I can now re-cognise as the sliding door being opened to allow me an entry to where I am today, happy and in love. Dots now connected.

Back away from the pain body

Some goodbyes set you free.
– Unknown –

Amidst the throes of the break-ups and the fights, but having learned already that evolution must have been happening (if only I could have seen it), along came the formidable Mr Eckhart Tolle, whose work I started to read and follow in my effort to move further along that evolutionary path. His teachings have been undoubtedly the single biggest influence on my resilience-building capability. I have read his books *The Power of Now* and *A New Earth* probably over ten times. His ideas and philosophies can feel extremely foreign at first and also intellectually challenging. But each time I read them (or listen to his strange yet soothing voice on a podcast), I get a new helpful construct that offers me a passageway towards greater self-sufficiency.

At the time and through trying to understand the reason why I could not make this relationship with Jake work, the most powerful and relevant snippet of knowledge for me was Tolle's discourse on what he calls the "pain body". In short, the concept is that we carry with us accumulated pain from past experiences that becomes lodged in our minds and bodies as a negative energy field. It can become active or be triggered by anything that resonates with a pain pattern from your past. For me, even the most innocent of remarks or a momentary absence of attention could activate it, and my partners throughout my life have no doubt borne the brunt of this extra-terrestrial body. Sometimes I would push the activation button my own damn self just for the attention and to justify, or explain away, my own uncharming behaviour.

Tolle's view is that unhappiness or discontent is often the awakening of the pain body and that over-identification with it can result in an aggressive and successful takeover bid on your life and the lives of others as it starts to live through you. Once that takeover has happened, you start to create situations in your life that vibrate on the same frequency and more pain is either experienced or, worse, perpetrated. I used to vehemently deny that I wanted such pain in my life and that it was all happening to me, without any contribution of my own or any ability to change it. The internal narrative was that I was, one hundred per cent, a victim of this pain body.

During this phase of my life, the best I was able to do was become aware of the pain body's existence and the havoc it could wreak on my life. That was about it, though. How to manage it successfully came later. Tolle's view is that the only thing that can assist you to dissolve this pain body is to shine the light of presence on it. He is very clear in his view that the pain body cannot prevail against the power of your own presence, which, of course, can be accessed and experienced through meditation, which I had not yet found the discipline to try (or at least stick to). His view is that if you can experience yourself as the observing awareness that is witnessing the pain body making appearances in your present moments, then you can release your identification with it as *who* you are and instead understand it as just an illusory construct carried forward from your past.

The truth of it was that I was just more comfortable in my pain body. I unabashedly used it to justify some of my outlandish emotional behaviour. Sitting pretty in my pain body, I didn't have to make the incredibly intense efforts required to move towards progress. I could actually just use the pain body as my excuse for remaining in the quicksand of my problems, constantly making tiny shifts with my feet to try to gain life momentum and escape but ultimately getting sucked back down again and again. But Tolle lit a fire in me that has never gone out. I saw the glimmers of sensibility in what he meant about the power of a laser focus on the present moment, of the uselessness of trying to change an unchangeable past and re-live it day after day even after it has stopped. But I just wasn't ready to fully let go and occupy the present moment. And my pain body continued to pop her head around the corner and say "peek-a-boo" for a few more years to come. Later in my life, I did find ways to close that door in her face, but she still creeps in every now and then to say hello.

Sometimes when both people in a relationship carry the heavy loads of their own respective pain bodies, you also start to see the commencement of epic battles about whose is the biggest. It becomes a game of "my pain is bigger than your pain", with constant justifications for our bad behaviour based on the magnitude of how messed up we feel, how agonised we were by the past pain inflicted upon us by others.

But the continued path of awakening saw me start to move more furiously towards any new advice, information, course – anything that could see me heal in some small way and become more present. I didn't want to be a victim to this pain body anymore. I wanted control back. The direct opposite of self-sufficiency is neediness, and so it is something I continue to strive every single day to overcome just a bit more than yesterday. I want my happiness to be measured by how I feel about myself when I am by myself, not by how some man is viewing me.

Sure, it has been such a beautiful addition to my life finding my husband and to be fortunate enough to love and love deeply. But the key learning for me at this point in my life is to continue to aspire to be able to have an enduring relationship without the rigid attachment, or at the very least with more confidence that, if my husband did at any point decide to leave, I would still be OK on my own. This doesn't mean putting up protective barriers that prevent the formation of connection and unity. It's about not solely relying on that love from another in order to be fulfilled but rather having that love operate as if it were icing on an already delicious cake. It was time to start learning how to be most happy with me. The person we will spend the longest period of time with on Earth is, after all, ourselves.

Don't try to change people

The cautionary tale in relationships is, of course, when one person starts to change in a more positive direction for themselves and the other stays comfortably stuck in their own mud. I have learned that the absolute worst thing you can do at this point (or any point, really) is to try to change them. First of all, it's actually a form of manipulation. And second of all, it's damn exhausting. Who am I to say that my way is the glorious high way? It might, for the other person, be the highway to hell. And if someone is showing no self-motivation to change, why would I use all my efforts to seek to invoke that rather than invest all that energy into my own growth? Is my desire to change someone else avoidance of facing what I need myself to in order to evolve? Or could it be a projection of my own self-image onto another? These are all questions that have come up in my life and in relationships when I have tried to change a partner.

I know from experience that my own change has never come as a result of being whipped into it by someone else. In fact, when someone does pull out that whip, even if I know in my heart that they are right, the stubborn streak of defiance creeps in and I recoil, crying "Abuse! Abuse!" For those rare times that I allowed the lashing and advanced on the suggested change management course, it never lasted. Quite simply because I was not self-motivated. I need to believe that change and adaptation is what is required myself before it has a real hope of being effective and lasting. I need to have experienced the hard whack from the life baton myself, or at least see one coming my way, to move most triumphantly in the direction of personal metamorphosis. The domain of change is a scary place to be. It is a little bit like an unknown limbo land between where you are now and where you want to be, without knowing what you are passing through or how you will get there. No one wants to be pushed into that dark city by someone else. They need to enter confidently with their own internal flicker of light guiding them.

My attempts to change partners have swung between gargantuan requests to change the total essence of who they are to smaller, but no less petty, appeals. To a quiet, introspective man, *would you be so kind as to be a tad more extroverted and social, please?* Easy. To a depressed person, *do you think you could smile once in a while and not be so negative?* Simples. To someone who has never needed to see a doctor in their life, *I genuinely wish you would be healthier and exercise more like I do, my dear.* Yeah, that makes sense. And to a historical-fiction-loving *Game of Thrones* devotee, *could we just stop with that aggressive nonsense, please, and watch Prince Harry talk about mental health for a moment?* Obviously a far better way to spend life. Nothing to see here. All totally reasonable behests for such obvious and necessary change, right? These last two examples are just sheer self-serving arrogance, but when I find myself trying to change more quintessential elements of who a person is, it is time to ask myself *why* I am doing it.

I told myself for so many years that if a partner was depressed then I could save them. I would even sometimes romanticise it as the destined reason why we were to meet. Out would fly Sarah the Superhero from the phone booth to save the day. Not only was it a distraction from the self-work clearly requiring initiation, it made me feel good about myself. It made me feel like my lovers' very own lionheart. Of course, if you see a partner suffering in any way, your very good intentions are to try to save them, to reduce their pain. What loving person would not do that? But these days I now ask myself, before I charge forward like a possessed army general, *did they ask me for my help?* If not, I try to softly retreat (oftentimes against my own natural will).

If someone is not asking for help and doesn't even want their problems solved, or just feels more comfortable without the pressure of your "higher state" hovering over them, then no matter how pristine the intentions might be, when you try to offer advice to them, it can often be perceived as a hostile mental takeover bid or, a tad less dramatically, you taking the moral high ground. It does put a dividing layer of separation between you. You as the expert on one side of the partition and them as the stupid idiot student on the other. No doubt, I have seen in myself and in others the wearing of suffering as an award, the public pinning of pain onto our lapels to demonstrate our ninja-warrior-level prowess at agonising endurance challenges. But more often than not, someone in this stage of development is looking more for acknowledgment of their efforts to get on with life despite the throbbing aches, or empathic confirmation about how difficult it must be for them.

Ultimately, people do not want solutions exacted on them when they are just not ready. I have in the past annoyed not only my partners but myself, too, with my tendency to get on a new bandwagon and then try to convince everyone to get on it with me. I probably repelled people, rather than inspired them, as I enthusiastically sprung off my spiritual trampoline in bouncy flight towards my latest enlightenment expedition, encouraging people to leap with me. But the truth of the matter is that I should have just done it, done it for myself and myself only, and for no kind of self-aggrandisement. If that action by me and its visible impact on my own life then had the Pied Piper effect of inspiring a following of any kind by a partner away from their own pain pandemic, at least it would have been an independent choice rather than a third-party compulsion.

I have heard this alternative paradigm of influencing others very romantically referred to as being a light post, a beacon, an exemplar. And when growth and happiness illuminate in you as a result of your own focus on just you, perhaps it will organically inspire the other to sway that way themselves. It kinda makes logical sense that change is more lasting when it comes around as a result of one's own choice and effort.

The benefits and growth that come about from this kind of light-post inspiration, rather than forced change, can be so beautiful. My husband, who is more introverted than me, has told me that he has taken inspiration from aspects of my personality and lifestyle that felt foreign but appealing after having seen their positive effect on me and others, like spending more time with friends or giving back to the community. And he changed as a (natural) result. I, too, an extreme requirer of thanks and praise, have adopted change towards more unconditional giving, having seen the profound impact this can have on the recipient, and my husband's inner peace. All of this from simply observing him be more anonymous and un-expecting when he does kind things. Win-win.

You cannot change or mould a person into a person that will fulfil you. As hard as it might have felt, turning the mirror around to face myself and commence the inner work that started to lead me towards my own independent fulfilment was a smart move. If I can find that, if I can work on that, if I can make even tiny incremental movements towards it, then it is that which I can release into my relationships to inspire any necessary change. If, ultimately, after all of that, we don't meet at the same corner of Evolutionary Street, then nobody should do what I did after my major life-changing break-up. Which was to chase my partner down the street screaming at him, and anyone in my life who was standing on their front lawns as I megalomaniacally passed by, that the idiot had taken the wrong damn path.

Instead, I wish I had just harmoniously withdrawn my expectation of a high yield. I should have turned off the flow of energy I was misdirecting towards my ex, minimised the amount of toxic hatred and negativity sent his way and simply stopped feeding the past any more attention. It would have been far more sensible to repurpose that attention for inner good and try to joyfully let it go. The lesson here: try as hard as you can not to turn your nose up as you leave. Easy for me to say, when I have categorically failed to do that, but a girl's gotta grow.

Look for an alliance, not a relationship

All this talk about change has changed me. While there was a time in my life when I craved totally enmeshed symbiotic love formations between me and another, now I look for more space. Not distance, just safe amounts of space to create my own dreams and work on my own issues but while also being lovingly supported. Kahlil Gibran says it most beautifully in his poem "On Marriage":

> *But let there be spaces in your togetherness,*
> *And let the winds of the heavens dance between you.*
> *Love one another, but make not a bond of love:*
> *Let it rather be a moving sea between the shores of your souls.*
> *Fill each other's cup but drink not from one cup.*
> *Give one another of your bread but eat not from the same loaf.*

To think that these progressive words were published in 1923 is just mind-blowing to me. The foresight he had on what are essentially modern and liberal relationship concepts is divine.

I have come to learn from my relationship experiences that having points of difference between myself and my partner doesn't have to be divisive. It doesn't mean I have to set about changing them to be more like me. If that were so, I may as well just go and stand in front of a mirror and love myself into eternity. I believe that even with sprinkles of difference dust, a relationship can still be unifying. It is not about trying to change someone so that they give you more of what you want to see. It is about being willing to surrender your own preferences in favour of what the other might want from time to time in order to bind you more closely. If what your partner does and the way they live their life does not engender the ability or the inclination to offer that kind of renunciation of your preference for theirs, then it may well be time to decide whether they are right for you after all.

Everyone deserves the loving support they need to fulfil their own desires. Everyone deserves the comfort of having someone join them for their ride. The word *relationship* does refer in the dictionary to the way two or more people are connected, but we all know that you can be connected by blood or connected by nationality and that does not necessarily mean it is a positive connection. In one knowledge course I completed, the teacher made a salient point that Iraq and Iran are in a relationship but that does not necessarily mean it's a positive thing. In that same very point, he offered me my own relationship "a-ha" moment: that we should aspire less to relationships and more to *love alliances.* An alliance, by definition, is a union or association formed between two or more people, just like a relationship, but it goes that one step further and is a relationship for *mutual benefit*, one based on similarity of interests, nature or qualities rather than just the mere state of being joined. I want more of those in my life. More love alliances, please, for everyone.

CHAPTER THREE

Guru Society

Re-examine all you have been told at school or church or in any book, dismiss whatever insults your own soul, and your very flesh shall be a great poem.

– Walt Whitman –

Who is this Guru, Lord Society, that I speak of here? Unlike our parents and our partners, a society is not a person on whom we can rely to remove darkness from our lives. But make no mistake about it, Guru Society is still capable of being worshipped in a way that seeks to derive or influence our own sense of who we are. And is a Guru often looked to as a source of information that we mistakenly use to put the "fill" in fulfilment. Society says, put your hands on your head. And most of us do. I have used societal "norms" to fill up my own mental cup of what is good and what is bad, what is acceptable and what is not. Not just in my own individual mental constructs but also to assess and judge the actions of others within that same society. I am not talking about organised and voluntary associations of individuals who form micro-societies for common ends, beliefs or professions here. Not The Law Society. Or The Literary Society. People who join these societies choose to become members to interact and pursue already-established common goals.

No, I am talking more about the broadest possible type of society. A group of unique people living together in an organised way. The collection of people and institutions around us. There are the narrower concepts of society that are localised and for whom the grouping shares the same geographical or social territory and those within it are subject to the same political authority and dominant cultural expectations. But there is also the broader global society, which I like to think of as humankind, society-at-large. In this globally networked, web-based world that we live in, societal influence, messaging and expectations can be felt from just about anywhere and from just about anyone. Parents, leaders, companies, teachers, even total strangers on the internet. They all have an opinion about who we are or should be. And we are exposed to all of it, all of the time and from a very young age.

I have been an avid devotee of society, or prominent figures within it, to varying degrees over time. Those influences over me have been both immensely good and immensely bad, and they continue to be. But through that devotion, I have learned some really valuable nuggets of wisdom that propelled me further towards greater self-sufficiency.

Ego, meet Society

> *Maybe there is nothing wrong with you. Maybe it's just really difficult to exist within a system that was not designed to support a spirit like yours.*
>
> – Unknown –

We are champions at assigning ourselves a whole lotta labels. I am this, I am that. Some complimentary, others just plain mean girl stuff. I commenced my own spiritual investigation very early on, to try to understand who this "I" was that was spending so much time in, and soaking up the norms of, the society in which I found myself. It was on this exploratory trail that I met my not-so-good mate Ego. Unfortunately, the ego is an occupant in everybody's minds and lives, but I was always curious to know a bit more about just what it was and why its presence in my life felt so wildly dictatorial.

The way that I like to describe the ego, to anyone not patient enough to listen in full, is that it is simply our mind-identified and intellectually created sense of self. It is the concept of ourselves as a person, with a very specific past and future, that we proceed to describe based on the adoption of commonly used identifying labels such as the place we were born, the job we have, or the person who birthed us (or that we birthed ourselves). I am Sarah, an Australian lawyer, daughter of Judith and Michael, mother of Stella. Ego is that layer of our consciousness that starts to assemble its identity, as it exists in relation to our physical form and body, from our very first day on earth. And it doesn't stop. At a ferocious pace, it takes in continuous cues from the outside world, such as what physical attributes or personality traits we have or have been told that we have by others. I am Sarah, a good girl, a sensitive girl, a blonde girl, a talkative girl, a passionate girl. Ego is essentially any image you have of yourself (or that has been imposed on you by others) that gives you a sense of outward identity.

Now go ahead and introduce Ego to Society. And there you have it, a pairing that makes for a dangerous, dangerous love affair. Together, their power to limit who you *really* are is, in fact, limitless. All you gotta do is lump your big old pain body on top of them and it can seriously start to feel like there is no way out from underneath the heavy load. You could almost define the ego as a harmful side effect of society. Or, conversely, try to imagine society as you would a social media influencer and the ego as a devoted follower. Your identity is undeniably shaped by the extent to which your ego allows society, or anyone in any part of it, to inform or define who you are. Because, let's face it, even for the most evolved human being, the waves of societal pressure are hard ones to surf sometimes. And, more so, some are of such tidal force that they are hard to let break on the shore of your soul without experiencing any level of cold or dampness at all.

Slowly but surely, as time continues to tick, our egos get populated with a vast number of experiences, ghostly remnants of the past and copious extraneous opinions and messaging, all of which come to mould the way in which we understand not only ourselves but others too. Our sense of self is therefore being curated by "other". The combination of ego and society creates an indelible imprint for how we see and go into the world. And what, then, has been created? I would say, at best, an indoctrinated individual. I know I am one. My exploration since coming to understanding this has been to start to observe more closely how this phenomenon has impacted my life and, more so, ask *what am I going to do about it?*

As a young adult, I found it difficult to comprehend who the "I" was that was even aware of the ego and society doing all the dangerous and indoctrinating labelling. This understanding came later in my life. But I knew enough to know that this was worth exploring more. I, whoever that turned out to be, was definitely onto something. My sense of who I was started to feel as though it could be much bigger, much more expansive and unlimited, than my ego was having me believe.

Seek first to understand the other. Be open to changing your mind.

> *Your capacity to allow people to live a truth completely opposite to yours, without shutting off your compassion for them, is a reflection of how powerful your love is.*
>
> – Unknown –

We need to operate in a society. This is an unavoidable fact of life. The question top of my mind, as I continue to try to do so, is *how can I do that more peacefully? How can I do that without my own happiness being at the whim of its grand and influential presence?* There are so many wonderful benefits of being a member of society if it is operating in a truly respectful and communal way. We are relational beings, after all, and can play an invaluable role in helping each other to survive. A healthy, supportive interdependence can sometimes be a good thing. I have found, though, that society has a remarkable capability in that it can be as separatist as it can be binding. It can band people together with as much might as it can rip them apart. I get disappointed when societal connectivity is elevated only when people can sniff out likeness and mutuality in the other. Or when societal segregation manifests at the first sign of difference or dissent. My heart rate elevates when I see any kind of ostracism of a person to the cold outer rims of the society we live in just because they have a different worldview, and usually a minority one. The ego, paired with society, has the tendency to create a world based on separate bodies, separate needs and a hierarchy of order in which some members deserve abundance and other's do not.

I have come to believe that we could go a long way towards mending this separation if we all just tried to understand each other better before we judged. And then, upon having attained that deeper grasp, if we also had a willingness to have our minds changed. This blessing made its way towards me as I started to became more conscious of how many times a day that I would so resolutely say things like "These politicians are all such useless morons – who on earth would make such a decision?" or "Gosh, my friend is such a fool for doing that." Or about public figures in society whom I did not even know personally, casting unrequested opinions to others who did not know them either, about choices they were making or activities they were engaged in.

I started to become much more aware of how often this kind of critical and ferocious teardown happened on the news, in social media, at work, at family events and even just around the dinner table with friends. We are all doing it. Everyone seems to have a view on how that other person has behaved or the actions that they take. Lucky for those being judged if that assessment is positive, but lord hear your prayers if you happen to be on the flip side where the view is predominantly disparaging or fault assigning. In my early years, I used to engage in this kind of judgement without a second thought. I could even go so far as to say that I loved nothing better than a "good goss" or providing an oral opinion piece on other people's lives.

In the beginning, there were less remorseful tugs of self-awareness and clear wins for my ego over kindness based on its ingrained system of conditioned beliefs. But as I did more and more self-work and became aware of the volume of judgemental thoughts I was having (or, worse, expressing out loud), it started to feel like a creeping vine of shame and guilt entangling itself around my soul. Sometimes the grip of that vine was so tight it would come close to choking me either into self-shame if I was the opinion orator or disappointment in others if they were dishing out the vitriol. I started to realise that the more we seek to blame others or things outside of ourselves, the more we are just relieving ourselves of the responsibility to take action, as if life is someone else's responsibility.

So, I started to catch myself more ahead of time or give myself some stern talkings-to afterwards if it was too late and I had already blurted it out. I am not saying it is not OK to ever have an opinion or observe and consider the behaviours of others. But I try now to be more curious than I am judgemental. Each time I feel disapproval of others arise within myself, I now try to approach my analysis of it with the spirit of enquiry, rather than judgement. I must admit, as a very opinionated person it has taken a few attempts at catching myself, but it is ultimately making for a nicer version of me.

Nothing incites the likelihood of civil unrest in a society like the removal of individual freedoms. Globally, we all saw that in 2020–21 with the COVID-19 lockdown periods. This new promise to myself to try curiosity before criticism was challenged. Big time. But I became more motivated to do it justice once I started to see the damaging effects of judgement over compassion during this unprecedented societal crisis. At points the judgement felt like it was completely inhibiting any movement towards progress or conciliation.

First it was the constant hate speech and blame towards our politicians, who I am pretty sure did not have "manage a global health pandemic" on their CVs before making their way into office. I acknowledge that they have leadership duties which they agree to take on, but before we cast our blame nets over their dear heads, I did find myself wondering whether anyone had stopped to ask them what their personal lives had become during the pandemic. How intense must it have been to make fast calls on such serious risks affecting so many people? What kind of other challenges were they facing when making pressurised decisions of this magnitude? The question troubling me the most was had we showed enough compassion to make our government representatives feel safe enough to make tough and unpopular decisions for the sake of our health and safety?

Then there was the serious condemnation of anyone who didn't wish to get vaccinated. I remember one newspaper story about a group of protesters who rallied against restrictions which used the words "selfish boofheads", "rebels with no idea", "clowns" and "half-wits" – all within the space of one paragraph. I would have given anything to hear a balanced interview or seen the initiation of a community forum on the topic so that I could truly understand why the anti-vaxxers thought vaccinations were not safe or what other personal reasons they may have had to explain their reticence. Whilst many of those reasons might have been irrelevant considerations for others, we could have at least asked them before we overthrew them into societal shame and oblivion. I may not have changed my own mind to vaccinate, but it would have at the very least expanded my own knowledge base and given divergent thinking a safer landing pad.

Did the meania, oops, my bad, the *media* seriously think that calling the vaccination protestors all those horrible names would drive them towards where most of us wanted them to go, which was safely indoors? Au contraire. Surely history has taught us enough times that hatred incites more of the same. I know there were many in these protesting groups that acted inexcusably violently towards innocent and heroic police officers and may well have been there to cause trouble and grandstand, but in that same footage I also heard real human beings, suffering, that wanted to be understood. One man shouted that the $600 concession that the government had gifted him simply wouldn't feed his family.

I remember at the height of the coronavirus period jumping into an Uber one day. The driver was quietly shaking his head as he listened on his radio to the same kind of hateful media commentary that pre-judged rather than giving comprehension a go. They were reporting on removalists who had reportedly crossed borders while carrying COVID-19 as well in their truckloads. I asked him how he was doing. He told me that he had five children and that his wife had just given birth to a new bubba. He said that normally his family would have flown in from Jordan to gather around and support the sizeable brood. Without anger in his voice, just an immense sadness and a sense of serious deflation, he said that all he wanted was for one of the interviewers to walk up to one of the so-called "rogue removalists" and ask them *why* they did it. Ask them what it was about their life that caused them to take this dangerous risk. He didn't need to tell me what he thought that removalist might say. His sad eyes, above his masked face, told me without words. I got the point. Even if it would have turned out that the removalist was just an irresponsible rule breaker.

There is no doubt that cooperation is a core element of a highly functioning society. But so is a healthy amount of well-managed conflict. Through debate, where "opponents" seek to understand each other's divergent points of view, can come a closer sense of real community but also innovation and more advanced evolutionary change. George Bernard Shaw expressed it so beautifully when he said that "Progress is impossible without change, and those who cannot change their minds cannot change anything."

Positive change in either our individual lives or, better yet, in the world is hampered if it is approached with a dogmatic point of view that one refuses to take their mitts off. I have always been persuaded by the theory that human beings, by their nature, can sometimes find it hard to allow their engrained ego or society-driven beliefs to be destroyed by "facts" because for many people those beliefs define them and are a central component to their self-identity. To destroy those beliefs might to some equate to destruction of the self. And then what happens is that we attribute a gold-level value to any skerrick of information that protects these beliefs even if it is dead set untrue. I aspire now to have a mind that can open wide enough to allow for the possibility that there are things that I just don't know and that proactively seeks to find out what they are, which may not only make me smarter but could also bring me closer to other human beings. Bingo.

Is that so?

I once read a great book by Hans Rosling called *Factfulness: Ten Reasons We're Wrong About the World – And Why Things are Better than You Think.* Page after page, his intelligent data-supported words douse the reader with undeniable proven facts about international phenomena such as global poverty, epidemics, war and terrorism with the specific intent to challenge the negative and dramatic misconceptions that might be colouring our view of the world. He convincingly demonstrated how reliance on anything other than facts can skew our understanding of these phenomena into an unnecessarily negative mode. His book taught me about the need to remember that the way we interpret the world we live in is a very limited and personalised view influenced by so many others.

The best realisation I had when reading his book was that *thoughts* are not facts. Think about that for just a second. It is soooooooo liberating. Thoughts are just little stories we tell ourselves, and those stories are influenced by so much early conditioning and societal belief systems that we are told represent the truth.

I am trying, every day, to reduce my *suggestibility* – the ease with which my view can be managed by external stimuli. Or having society dictate to me what or who I think I am. For so long now I have operated my life as if one of The Monkees. A Believer. But a believer of too many other people and less of myself. If someone disparages me, I'm a Believer. If someone praises me, well, I'm a Believer too. *You're too emotional, Sarah.* Yeah, you're right. *Your emotions make you such a loving, kind leader, Sarah.* Hmmmm, also correct. *You need to set more boundaries for your daughter, Sarah.* Oh lord. You might be onto something there. *Oh, Sarah, you are such a liberal and progressive-thinking mum. Your daughter is so lucky.* OK, I change my mind. All aboard. First stop: Believer-ville. Next Stop: Sad Sacks City.

Once you board this train, it can change its timetable at any time, and just when you think you are heading to one destination, the driver, whom you have given control to, hits a button and you are on a new track once again, perhaps heading somewhere you didn't even want to go. And as you sit on that train staring blankly out the window, you stop seeing each view as a possible fresh perspective and instead all you see are views that confirm the limited outward-led opinions about who you are. Your mind becomes prejudiced by what you think or have been told is the truth about the world. So much so that everything you see or hear from that point on verifies it. What you are conditioned to believe starts to become more emphatic "truth", which can potentially distort your reality.

You think – based on what you see and hear more of as time goes on – that you are just collating rational evidence that proves you right. But really, you are only finding that evidence because you held that view in your awareness to begin with. In effect, you develop a cognitive bias towards noticing any kind of image or information that backs up the storyline created by the ego and society. I try hard to catch that little habit in my personal evolution mousetrap as often as I can, precisely so that I can pick the evidence apart a tad more consciously. Society can almost feel like a strengthening of tribal affinity, but the problem with that is that anything outside of the common set of beliefs or widely accepted behaviours then starts to feel like disobedience, deserving of personal punishment. And it should not. Any reliance on society, or the people within it, as the judge and jury on who we are and what we can handle is most definitely limited and requires courageous challenge if it doesn't feel right.

We know that the brain uses "existing models" from what we have seen or experienced before – that is how we develop this personalised world we walk around in. Everything we see with our eyes is actually just a mental construct. We live in a world of stimuli and we build models and explanations for sensory stimulus, which become nothing more than conditioned sensory responses. But we don't live in an absolute world where everyone agrees, do we? No, it is all relative depending on where you stand. Who is to say what is beautiful? Or what is painful? The experience of a rich equity banker in London might differ greatly to someone living below the poverty line in a developing country. The answer of a young child may vary significantly to that of a grown adult.

Each one of us is a great big collection of all our past experiences and influences. So, in our conversations with each other about what might technically be explained as the "same thing", we need to accept that each person's view of that "same thing" will be from their own unique perspective, past experience and history. And this lends weight to the argument (and very useful life reminder) that even when people disagree, or have alternative points of view, on that "same thing", neither of those two individuals is right or wrong. They are just experiencing life and applying meaning to it based on their own mental constructs developed over their own lifetimes.

I find the implication of fully understanding this rather exciting. What if all that we have been told is not even true and there are unlimited possibilities available to us that we are not aware of yet? What if I could expect even greater from the world than the limited experience of what I am seeing today? How would it feel to still see what is right in front of me but minus what it is I have been told to expect about that thing, person or situation? What if I gave myself permission to imagine for just a second that everything in the room that I am currently sitting in has no meaning and to remove the limited meaning I have given it? What happens then? Those doors on that train to Believer-ville just might open up to a whole new world of infinite destinations, possibilities and meanings that already exist but which I am yet to discover.

One of the most illuminating ways I have had this phenomenon described to me is to think of it in the same way as what happens when you watch a magician's trick. It is pretty common to feel totally and utterly bewildered because whatever you see before your very own eyes cannot be computed by your brain. The explanation for this reaction is that what just happened up there on the stage simply doesn't fit inside any existing model wired into your brain and so you cannot perceive it in reality. It remains as magic. Impossible. Even though it has literally just been done. It is the same with life. Just because we cannot envisage a new or more supportive reality for ourselves, that doesn't mean it doesn't (or cannot) exist. It probably just means we are yet to discover it and are limited in some way by our own minds. Just knowing there could be more to life than the meaning I had either inherited or arbitrarily given to it was enough of a starting point for me to begin to understand the perils of an over-reliance on what society and everyone in it tells me is right. And that there is a blinding force created by social hypnosis and cultural indoctrination that I want to start to break through.

There is a Buddhist teaching about the "don't know mind" that I keep tucked up in the back of my mental horsepower for when I need it. The Buddhist philosophy as I understand it is that we should aim to foster a beginner's mindset, meaning that you should assess any life situation, your own inner belief system and even someone else's idea or opinion with a mindset of simply *not knowing*. It is believed to open up the floodgates for new or creative ideas and more unity with others. This kind of mindset also naturally brings less judgement, more willingness to consider to new ideas and less bias towards a point of view that may not even be the truth or who you really are.

Adopting a don't know mind allows a closed or prejudiced mind to expand, and it also affords you more magic in everything that you see around you, almost as if you are seeing it for the first time. I have found utility in this idea and have reaped the benefits of adopting it in multiple areas of my life. In a work environment it has enabled me to stay innovative. And in my personal life it has enabled my relationships to become less volatile. All because this mindset allows the awareness and the space to genuinely consider the other persons point of view. Funnily enough, it has even worked for me when I am busy berating myself for being somehow useless or deficient. I am finding it more and more beneficial that every time I think I know something for absolute certain, I ask myself quietly *is that so?* Sometimes I answer with a defiant *hell yeah, it is!* and I dig my feet right on in, but every now and then when I am feeling less stubborn or irrational, a little room for another perspective is created, opening a tiny keyhole to evolution. And so, I grow.

Populate your mind with more of the good stuff and less of the bad

If our egos are busy soaking up all these layers that we add to our mental constructs, then I am coming to understand that I need to up my game so that I become a better security bouncer of my own mind. I need to get that door list ready with the names of what kind of images, thoughts and ideas that I will and won't let into my mental club. The low-level security system that I sometimes have safeguarding the entrance to my mind can make for a chaotic dancefloor. I need to upgrade that shit to operate more like a VIP exclusive establishment and keep the mental riff-raff out as best I can.

At risk of being called a naive scaredy cat, I am going to go ahead and admit something about myself that has been the subject of great debate and mild criticism by others in my life. I actively avoid, as far as humanly possible, without becoming totally ignorant and non-worldly, the mainstream news. And I flat-out refuse to watch a horror film. The loud gashing sounds on *Game of Thrones* offend my (very) delicate sensibilities. And only out of an attempt to maintain the love and affection of my husband can I watch a mildly dramatic action series on Netflix. And this is on a very strictly enforced condition that he either holds up the blanket when the shooting or body decimation begins or doesn't relay what transpired it if I deliberately leave to brush my teeth while it is happening. My husband, at worst, will turn his face one inch to the left if someone is being maimed and tortured. And that is probably because he is not an Anxious Annie like his good wife here.

Fact of the matter is, I don't like seeing bad things happen to people. But even if I really should pull up my scaredy cat socks and acknowledge the difference between non-fiction and fantasy, I am sticking to my game plan here. There is an abundance of research that has shown that for those who do already suffer from any kind of baseline (even mild) anxiety, watching horror films can heighten that anxiety, lead to mood disturbances and very interrupted sleep patterns, which is very damaging to your physical and mental health. Even though your rational brain may be aware that the threats are not real, your body registers them as if they are.

It is no different with the news. And today it feels like we cannot escape it. It is everywhere. A constant stream. And its tone is increasingly emotive. Its graphic imageries are often shocking, and its commentaries are mostly negative and laden with fear. Like horror films, there is also research that these kinds of repetitive, stressful stimuli cause the release of the adrenaline hormone, which cranks up the nervous system's flight or fight response, putting extraordinary pressure on the autonomic nervous system, leading to mood changes, anxiety, depression and even just unnecessary amplification of personal worries and associated thoughts. My husband will often tell me when watching a film, "it's just a movie, sweetie", but he cannot say the same for real-life news.

Yes, it might have been embarrassing on those rare occasions when, for instance, I overheard a conversation about someone I knew to be a super-hot colleague and chimed in with my two cents' worth about how ridiculously good-looking he is, only to learn that they were intelligently discussing the policies of a parliamentary shadow minister with the same name. No doubt it was. But for all those scholarly experts on current affairs, maybe I could challenge them to a duel over knowledge levels regarding other things like consciousness or community – two topics I could not study enough if I tried.

It comes down, at the end of the day, to what I personally choose to populate my mind with, and I have just found that populating it with more colourful sprinkles and less dirty dust is making for a happier, less anxious life. The further I traverse this path, the closer I get to a lowered baseline anxiety and the less my sense of ease is dictated by a good or bad news day. But even if I had no anxiety at all, I still believe that some level of buffer from, or less immersion in, constant negativity or horrifying storylines can only be a good thing. There are ways to stay up to date on the important headlines without soaking for far too many hours a day in the bloodbath tub.

I have also started to be more selective about what is a good and reliable source of truth for me. While I am far from being a conspiracy theorist, we all know there are many influences and controls sitting behind what is told to us and what is not. Sometimes it feels as if there is no motivation for the mainstream news to tell a story with a more balanced and accurate reality of what is happening as it won't make as riveting content. And fuelling an already hot societal fire with some sensationalised aggression can oftentimes feel quite self-serving because it creates more reportable news.

There might well be wisdom in shifting our attention away from the deliberately aggravating media streams about some of the world's worst problems and instead using our energy to participate in activities or engagements that promote the kind of unity, love and energy that could contribute to a circumnavigation away from the death and destruction we are seeing. It is not about denial of reality but rather about choosing to spend your time in a way that might make an actual difference to reality. I would love to see a positive-news-only channel one day instead of just the five-minute throwaways about a cute cub born to a lion at Taronga Zoo at the end of twenty-five minutes of disaster reporting. There is more good, more humanity and more progress going on in the world than our media is giving it credit for. I want to seek out, participate and surround myself with more of that.

Hello, is there anybody else out there?

I started this chapter by suggesting that the output of the intermingling between my ego and society was an indoctrinated individual. After coming to understand that this was true, I certainly started to take steps to seek to move beyond my own limited, personalised worldview, in both how I understood and treated others and how I gave meaning to my own world. I implemented some tighter controls on what I let into that sacred, impressionable space of my egoic mind. But a conversation had started in that very same mind. One that saw me decide to stop avoiding the percolating question that often ended in an answer I could not fully understand about who this person was that was having all these observations about myself. I started to be more relentless with this ego of mine and have more patience with my own enquiry about whether there was more to see – and if so, what – that my ego was perhaps not comfortable allowing me to.

Eckhart Tolle describes the ego as the physical and hard shell that separates you from your true and formless self. *Wait, there is two of me?* He explains that the physical body and the mind (occupied by an ego) exist in the relative world, while at the same time a more expansive, formless, unbounded version of who we are exists in the absolute world. The complicating factor in this message for me when I first tried to unpack it was that this formless higher self is not actually separate from anyone or anything else. We are all actually one indivisible field of energy. I mean, c'mon. How is anyone in a dualistic world going to wrap their heads around this truth? The living, breathing, experiential comprehension of this, other than as a mere intellectual construct, remained beyond me. But the concept was now very active in my air space. Even if you cannot quite understand it either just now, I hope it has at least got you thinking.

This seedling of the truth – that apparently all my life I had been both the person I was labelling as having certain features or personality traits and the person who was observing those thoughts – had well and truly started to grow. I was not just an individual in a society of seemingly separate bodies; we were also completely connected. This was enough of a teaser campaign for me to continue in my search. To see if this bigger version of me was hiding somewhere behind a curtain, yet to be revealed. And from that point I have liberated myself from, and expanded, my sense of identity well beyond that which society, and all that is contained within it, had given me. It was as if my own personal evolutionary games had well and truly begun.

CHAPTER FOUR

Guru Job

Never hang your self-worth on somebody else's hook.
– Sarah Susak –

I call hum-bullshit

I entered the full-time working arena straight after having completed a double degree in psychology and law. Choosing law over the helping profession led me initially into a somewhat displaced feeling starting with my very first gigs in private practice law firms. It became quickly apparent that the law firm was the water and I was the fish that seemed well and truly out of it. I stuck with it for a while because I just could not put my finger on what it was about the environment that had me feeling so dry and alien from my fellow spritely and exotic legal sea creatures. I tried really hard to swim well. I gave it my absolute all, but as the years went on the performance reviews became tougher (at one point, along the veins of "you need a vocational counsellor, my dear") and the disappointment in myself after years of dedicated study started to grow. I just knew in my heart and soul that I should be enjoying this more. I should be doing better than I was.

When I was young, I remember some primary school teachers' concerns about my lack of attention to detail and the relatively short span between my commencement of a task and losing interest. Of course, hypotheses were drawn about my questionable ability to focus for long periods, or even whether it was just sheer laziness. It is interesting to me how quickly we tend to run toward labelling these kinds of issues diagnostically. My adult career experience has taught me that this particular behaviour of mine was actually an early indicator of the importance of seeking the right environment to achieve optimal satisfaction and performance.

It was true (and remains true) that I have a distinct preference for searching for the shortcut. The more efficient way to reach the solution; the least arduous path towards it. What could be defined as impatience, flipped on its head, is also efficiency. I just did not see the utility of knowing how to do a long division when I had a Casio calculator right by my side that would compute the answer in nanoseconds and with minimal effort. And through my experience in law firms, I also learned that my so-called limited attentiveness was more often cut short if the topic of the day just wasn't up my alley.

This clear need for both speed and affection for the subject matter was, however, met when I moved away from law firms across to the in-house legal counsel waters working with leading global marketing brands like Colgate and Coca-Cola. When I made that move, I started to swim like a fish that was finally one with its ocean. The fast-moving consumer goods business, the sexy brands, the proximity to the decision making, the need for instinctive commercial advice without over-analysis all just suited me better, and I embarked on an exciting legal career that took me around the world from Sydney to Geneva to New York to Paris (I was lucky enough to live in the French capital for several years).

For such a long part of my career, I did not assign Guru status to my job. I never felt, hand on heart, that my identity was strongly tied up in it. At least not consciously. I had never been one to turn to my job or immerse myself in it as a way to avoid personal issues or overcome darkness. That kind of refuge was always sought by me in other things. Whenever I would go out socially or be in conversation with others, the very last thing I would think to talk about or bring up first was my life as a corporate lawyer. I had so many other things or issues that I preferred to discuss and that I was interested in sharing ideas on.

Oftentimes, after a couple of hours of having met a new person, the common "and what do you do?" question would fall into my lap, and upon disclosure I would get very surprised looks and reactions. Some even openly suggested that I was the very antithesis of the image they had conjured up in their minds of an alpha female corporate legal executive. I really didn't live much of my life consciously aware of any dependency on my job as necessary to fulfil my sense of self-worth. I recall various points, some during the supreme heights of my career, when I could convey a sense of lofty detachment from my job. I enjoyed it, yes. I gave it my passionate all, every day, for sure. But did it light my fire? Was it really who I thought I was? Would I care if it was not a part of my life or someone didn't think that I was really good at it? I hadn't thought so. But, boy, did that change.

Looking back now, I cannot say I did not feel inwardly proud as I took steps up the corporate ladder. And I can definitely admit to feeling a little propped up by my fancy job titles, spurred on by my unsolicited promotions, and a tad shinier from the glitzy sheen of the big global brands that I worked for. I just didn't think that my sense of self-importance was heavily reliant on them. Certainly not as reliant as I was on other Gurus' I had leaned on for self-love so far.

I didn't think rank or status really made a difference to who I thought I was or how I felt about myself. The soon-to-be-discovered foolishness of this belief had been made hardier by a fairly constant flow of employer validation over the course of my in-house legal career that became so common it had almost become the norm. I can see now how this steady stream of compliments, consistent rewards and promotions had lulled me into an accidental arrogance. And, because of their reliable presence, one that had never been tested. Of course, I received constructive and helpful feedback about my weaknesses along the way but never of the nature that I had to consider what my life or self-image would look like without the reassurance of my employer's love for what I do and how I contribute.

You know how they say that you don't realise how much you'll miss someone until they are gone? It was a little bit like that for me when I hit a fork in the, to date, relatively blissful road of my career and realised how very un-humble I actually was. How very, very hooked I was on the validation of my colleagues and managers to verify how very, very excellent I was at my job. How the corporate cachet and feeling of being respected by others did, in fact, really make a huge difference to how happy or sad I was. That life-crashing boulder rolled ferociously down my inner slippery slope only when that constant stream of certification from others dried up momentarily. It was only in the absence of the outward glorification by others and the removal of my prestigious rank by someone else that I realised how dangerously dependant I had become on both of these things.

Such were the tidings of a rather insidious corporate restructure in my mid-forties. There is nothing quite like a corporate restructure to shine a light on our individual expendability and replaceability and the dangers of tying our self-identity to our work. After almost twenty years "at the top", the remit of my job was suddenly changed. Strangest thing about the entire experience and all of the realisations that came with it was that my position was one of the very rare few in this giant restructure that was not officially restructured. My position did not actually get made redundant. In my employer's view, my role and income remained essentially the same and I should be happy with this. I was categorised through the use of some irritating corporate restructure lingo as a mere "Lift and Shift". Some more seemingly "minor" things changed, though. I reported now into someone who was previously my peer. *Awks.* My job title was not as senior sounding. *Say whaaaaat?* I was no longer the leader of a team of lawyers. *No, you didn't.* And, I was not on the senior most executive leadership team for our region anymore. *Your loss!!!* Angry, I unilaterally changed my status to "Lift and Shift and Miffed".

Mirror, mirror on the wall, whose self-confidence took a sudden fall? The colonisation of the belief I thought I had in myself at work from Rock Solid Island to No Man's Land was of Christopher Columbus proportions. I settled on this previously foreign shore and spent my first few weeks drowning in a seemingly bottomless chasm of self-doubt before I began the real exploration, the careful but curious scrutiny of why this new land felt so frightening to me and, as always for this little action Barbie, what I was going to do about it. Having been so convinced until this restructure happened that I was someone that would be so unaffected by any change to my own importance in the workplace, someone so apparently detached from their job and all of its trappings, I had to ask myself *why, then, did this relatively minor undressing leave me feeling so stark naked?* Turns out, I had been free-riding for years on the back of my employer's Harley, holding on for dear life as we drove along the work superhighway, placing my delicate self-worth totally in their hands as the driver. It only took one fork in the road for me to realise swiftly that this was a dangerous and disempowering strategy which had been working only because the route had, to date, been relatively scenic and satisfying.

I realised that my so-called detachment from the grandiosity of my role was enabled only by the confidence others had in me. Until this restructure, I never had any cause or reason to evaluate whether I also thought I was good at my job or whether the titles and formal positions made a difference to my own sense of fulfilment. I had no reason to discover these things on my own or tell myself I was good. Everyone else had been doing the job for me. I do not doubt that I must have had some modest estimate of my own contribution, but that is because everyone around me was so successful in helping me believe that I was a valued team member. Until the protective helmet was removed, until the simple titles and trimmings were taken away, I had no idea how much I had relied on them after all. Instructed by my own highly emotional reaction and the negative impact the changes that came with the restructure had on my happiness and sturdiness, it became abundantly clear that it just was not sensible to allow my job or my employer to be the driver of my journey towards happiness ever again.

The most glorious gift to come from this forced self-exploratory experience was delivered to me in the viewing *dis*pleasure I experienced while watching the ludicrousness of my space shuttle speed shift from stable to unstable. I had not had my title changed or my team removed because my employer had decided that I was not good at my current job or because my performance had taken any kind of plummeting nosedive.

If that had been the case, perhaps I would have understood with more empathy the sudden shallowness of my self-confidence stream. But the staggering truth was that literally the day before the restructure and changes were announced, I was in a blissful state of self-belief and calm confidence. The day after, not so much. What had happened between these two days to justify such a rapid personal devolution?

My CV, skills and experience remained exactly the same on both days. Yet the independent decision of a corporation, who very likely did not have me in their mind at all when they made decisions about a new global structure for their business, had me on my knees imploring something "out there" to re-verify my excellence again. That just cannot be good. It does not even make logical sense. Here I was, staring my ego directly in the face, its tongue poking out. *Ha,* it said, *I got you.* It was time, clearly, for me to call hum-bullshit and never rely on a job, an employer or a mere title for a toll-pass to happiness ever again.

Be cool at the cooler

> *You know what to do with tough cookies, don't ya?*
> *Dip 'em in milk.*
>
> – Ted Lasso –

Discovery of the importance of independent inner belief can reap ravishing rewards in the domain of difficult people. Self-love can act as an invisible shield from the uninvited attacks of others. We all know they are out there. And in the workplace, where you are especially constrained by the need to employ bipartisan-like political strategies even when you have opposing points of view, difficult people, or even just nice people that don't particularly like or value you, can really challenge your stability.

We have all experienced that sinking sensation that comes with someone unnecessarily picking holes in your good work. Or that feeling of self-shame that shrouds an already mediocre day when your work is ferociously highlighted, and with fluorescent markers, by someone who wants to add extra emphasis to your blunders so that everyone can see them. Then there is that bitter disappointment that comes when someone you have lovingly supported at work does not return the loyalty. For me, relationships and their importance have always trumped ambition. But tying my happiness to the validation of a difficult person at work has made for some very tiring, anxious and, quite frankly, wasted days.

If nothing else, I try at a minimum to remember that a difficult or unkind person is a grand and free lesson in how not to behave myself. But if you work closely with someone day in, day out, being awarded a degree in how to behave better is not the most satisfying bridge over troubled waters. Some perfect but impractical advice I have been given about finding oneself in a difficult work entanglement is to simply remove yourself from the situation. Easier said than done if you work closely together. An alternative concept which negates the need for physical distance is to instead establish more emotional distance from said colleague.

But successful use of this technique can be totally inhibited if you, like I did at the time, have a need to be liked by others and held in high esteem. One challenge for me in the past was that I always wanted to be friends with everyone, and I would stop at nothing to make friendship the outcome of coming together with others in the workplace. I tried *way* too hard. And wild disappointment always followed when it was not reciprocated. Sometimes impacted quality time with my family or friends could result, distracted by my obsession with how mean someone was being or why they didn't rate me on the leader board of fabulous human beings.

But after having had enough of prolonged dismissive and disloyal treatment by one particular difficult person in the workplace, I gave this approach a go. Hard as it was for me, as unnatural as it felt, I emotionally distanced. I maintained full professionalism and candour about the work conversation and interactions but stopped sharing myself on a personal level and stopped dishing out possibly undeserved kindness in expectation for kindness in return. Instead of emotionally reacting to how they were making me feel, like crying or making myself vulnerable, I accepted the fact that they were not doing anything other than being themselves.

It was me who was allowing their view of me to implode my own. The words of author Wayne Dyer rang loud in my ears, reminding me that how someone treats me is their path but how I react is gloriously all mine. Instead of reactivity, I simply retreated – pulling up the defensive drawbridge on my own confidence castle. I am pretty sure I left the person wondering about why they had isolated themselves. Gave them space to question themselves while I also looked within. There is a great quote by Brendon Burchard that turned my commonly used strategy to kill mean colleagues with kindness on its head: "Toxic people will not be changed by the alchemy of your kindness. Yes, be kind, but move on swiftly and let life be their educator."

But, of course, it goes well beyond just psychologically distancing yourself from difficult people. Such disconnection was of no use to me if I could not also find a way to cease performance managing myself solely against what other people say. I have had to learn to accept that not everyone is going to see my value in every environment or context. I had to back myself. If someone at work would ever put me down, challenge my confidence or just flat out insult me, I started to ask myself is *the person directing their opinion towards me someone I look up to, admire or respect? Is there any utility I can extract from what they are saying?* If either of those questions had affirmative answers, I would most definitely use their input as an opportunity to grow and progress. However, if it was out of the mouth of a difficult or particularly unkind person who I had no aspiration to emulate, I would place less value on and pay less attention to what they had said and silently wish them my emotional farewell. It ain't easy, but I do try very hard each and every day not to let someone who doesn't know my true value tell me how much I am worth.

The space and sense of perspective gained from my emotional retreats did allow me to see interactions more clearly for what they were and less as ego-created personal attacks on me. There have been so many situations where my interpretive dance on top of what were mere neutral facts have turned a relatively boring short story into an epic blockbuster. It is the latter inflation that creates the suffering. And it is the former that, if I can stick to it, helps with the whole "move on" thing.

With more life experience, there came a time when the inner thought *that person believes my opinion on that matter was wrong and expressed that opinion to another person* seemed a lot less likely to impinge on my personal wellbeing than *that stupid asshole dared to challenge my astute technical expertise and yeeeeeaaaaaarrrrrrrs of untarnished experience and sold me out to my manager purely to make me look bad and get ahead for themselves.* Or, in observing the behaviour of difficult people towards my work besties, the thought *that woman is raising her voice at my workmate* is sure as hell less conducive to drama than *that cow needs to head out to pasture before I release some angry bulls out of the gate.* It could well be that the latter responses in both of these scenarios were perfectly fitting and a precise analysis of the situation, but maybe they are also just the overly emotionally laden stories I tell myself. Maybe one is right and one is wrong, but in many ways it would all become irrelevant if I could nuzzle my way into a position where my self-belief was so solid that I could see criticism or obstructive behaviours for what they are and not turn them into an exaggerated exposés.

Creating these static, one-dimensional, frozen-in-time versions of people also doesn't leave the room required for possible change in the other. I have been amazed by how much less seismic the dispersal of other people's anger down my own inner drainpipes has been when I am more certain about myself. And how much more unity is possible when I leave some open space in my heart for change in the other instead of condemning them to the one version of themselves that I do not seem to like today.

I will say that any attempt at retaliation or reverse criticism has always backfired for me. If not from the ongoing rapid-fire combat, then always from the sheer disappointment in myself that would never fail to rebound with more force than the original slap. There is no joy in lowering yourself to the level of someone with bad intentions. As Michelle Obama wisely counsels, when they go low, we go high. There has been no amount of my incessant whinging about someone else's behaviour, or spraying my negativity about that person to anyone whom I had voluntold to listen, that has ever decreased the very negativity that I was busy championing being removed. Nope, I was just adding to the crappy behaviour cesspool that I was simultaneously busy berating.

I have found it so curative of my anger towards others to keep the words "only hurt people hurt people" firmly imprinted on my mind. It's always sensible to stop for a second in the heat of any moment and ask myself *what is it that could be making that person act this way? What might be happening in their lives that has generated such intense reaction to my seemingly benign activity?* We can all only do as well, act as well and think as well as our level of consciousness will allow. My actions, while innocent to me, may be a severe trigger for another. If someone feels the need to criticise or hurt me, what I am really getting is a direct report on their level of consciousness. And even more powerful and confronting to consider or accept: if I were them, I would do exactly what it is they are doing.

Accepting this fact as true, even if counter-intuitive, provides me with an enormous opportunity to turn dislike, anger and separation into an experience of empathy and unity. Could I muster enough spirit to imagine how I might act if I was that person with that upbringing and history, that set of life experiences, that particular bad day? And could they do the same for me when I next unleash? Is it possible to imagine a world where, put in another's shoes, we might act as they do? This approach has enabled me to try as hard as I can to shift my focus to what might be nice about the person who is challenging me and away from those features which are driving me daisy. I refuse to believe that people can be all bad. What would it take for me to adjust my focus to catch a glimpse of any of their finer qualities or, more simply, what is right in front of me rather than what's in my head?

I have always wondered why, as humans, we find it so hard to recognise the unique value of every individual within a collective and come to know and appreciate just how wonderful that variation, in fact, is. The antidote to the tall poppy syndrome in a workplace context was gifted to me by one leader I had the pleasure to work for, who said that we need to establish the habit of what he called "talking people up behind their backs". I thought that was just genius. In teams and in broader work environments, for some odd reason, it is common to see people taking pleasure from watching others fail and/or finding the success of others in some way threatening. Ultimate work nirvana from a happiness and work productivity point of view, if I follow his thinking, is a place where everyone spends their time talking about and celebrating others' successes, standing proud alongside their colleagues and learning from each other. He was right when he said that this was an entirely countercultural aspiration, but I think that it is the direction we should all be heading.

There is a great quote I once read that spoke to this new phenomenon in my working life, that "until it's my turn, I'll keep clapping for others". My all-time favourite workmate and I established a wonderful practice when we worked together which we called The Jolt. The word *jolt* connotes just the right tone of violent movement and abrupt speed with which a jolt must be spurred towards the co-worker you wish to receive it. The rules of the game are that as soon as you have a good or positive thought about another person or their achievements at work, you have to, without thinking and with absolutely no editing, immediately send that expression of adoration to the other. You cannot second guess yourself, you cannot hesitate. And it has to be written or told in a way that will strike the other person in an electrifying manner. Gosh, we generated some powerful confidence conductance over the years. It is a practice that I have extended well beyond the workplace ever since, and I do it whenever and however I can.

Let the see-saw do its thang

> *Do you know why birds sing in the morning?*
> *Because they don't have to go to fucking work.*
> – Unknown –

One little blessing that I took from my time spent misusing work as a bow to wrap up my identity was my ability to start to find an answer to what has become a universal but almost rhetorical question of how one is expected to achieve work-life balance. Addressing this question has felt at times like I have been wearing a lab coat, making regular and varied observations about the problem, experimenting with different hypotheses, testing and trying new methods and just hoping for at least one of the many theories to stick. All the while I was holding out for that one research paper that would turn into a published peer-reviewed and accepted Nobel prize-winning scientific article that contained an actual and verifiable conclusion on the topic.

I could bestow upon myself the title of chairman of author Robin Sharma's 5 AM Club, such is the level of commitment I have to my membership and my unwavering belief in the revolutionary benefits I have received from gifting myself, after reading his book on the topic, a quiet hour of me-time before the family rear their heads and we all head to work for the day. And during my course of research on the topic of work-life balance, I have drawn inspiration from Sharma's idea that we should not decide what to do based on how much time we have, which will always feel limited, but rather whether something is, or should be, a priority.

But in my humble view, it is the actual damn term that everyone is trying to achieve, *work-life balance*, that is the crux of the problem. It already prescribes what the goal is. Balance. Making us feel that if we don't get balance, we have failed to reach the Golden Arches of the working human. And so, the constant and rhythmic *alas, woe is me, I have no work-life balance, I am a failure at everything I do in life* dance begins. More problematically, this turn of phrase predetermines, before one even starts to dream up ways to achieve it, that balance is, in fact, the right aspiration. But what if balance, an equilibrium between work and life, is just not at all what we should be trying to obtain?

That leaves a couple of other options. We could tip the scales in favour of the most important of the two and leave them there. Give eternal priority to the most crucial. You hear this adage often. That life, health and family are all that matters at the end of the day, and never have truer words been spoken. But how practical, realistic or helpful is that for the woman who, for example, might be a single mum with two kids, a mortgage and school fees trying to just put good food on the table? It leaves her with the job of deciding which one is the priority. It seems so obvious, but let's be real it is really, really easy to say and impossibly hard to do. More self-imposed zero out of tens. What if we could accept that balance is impossible, stop trying to achieve it and just give precedence to whatever of the two is more important or necessary in each particular moment?

Think about a see-saw. As one side goes up, the other side naturally and *effortlessly* goes down. The goal of the see-saw ride is the direct opposite of balance. It is absolutely not to try to stabilise it, with both sides levitating in space, inert and with no movement. That would not be fun; that would not be in the spirit of the see-saw and all the playful excitement it can bring. What if we could accept and recognise that, just like a see-saw, the weight of life and work may vary from day to day or week to week. And that we just need to stop assessing that imbalance as a failure and more like the execution of the classic playground ride – up and then back down again, on repeat.

One day your work and team may not get the best of you because your family has lumped itself on the other side of the see-saw with lofty importance. And there may be a week where a work project is of such passionate proportions, and one that you have worked so hard for and want to sink your teeth into, that your family will just have to cope with the grass dump. From the perspective of the see-saw, that's normal, that's fun, that's play. Certainly a more positive and supportive framework than the impossible art of the balancing act that only circus artists can really ever dream to achieve anyway. Could we just let the see-saw do its thang?

I don't want to make it sound super easy, but, then again, I kind of also do. Don't get me wrong, a playlist of the mixed tape of my own mind as it relates to thoughts and suffering associated with the pursuit of work-life balance would look a bit like this:

> *No Breaks Today, Don't Get Frustrated, Eating Meals is Overrated*
>
> *Just One More Midnight Zoom, It's OK, I Can Sleep in My Tomb*
>
> *Should Meet That Deadline, You Really Oughta, But Don't Forget You Have a Daughter*
>
> *Look At This Career I've Built, Why Do I Feel Such Crushing Guilt?*
>
> *Self-Care, Are You Really Out There? I'll Get to You One Day, I Swear*

My Albatross Boss

Oh, What A Career, Shame My Marriage Took A Bum Steer

You Got Yo' Wealth, But You Ain't Got No Health (Remix)

There is no doubt it takes courage to make decisions about what it is you will let fall and what it is you will allow to rise. And, yes, it will take a tuned-in intuitive mental acuity to make quick on-the-spot assessments of the risks associated with pushing your feet off the ground to spring something upwards to take its place at the top. I don't have a skerrick of doubt that while up there you will feel the pain and guilt associated with the rattling pressure of the thing or person on the other side applying some force to try make its way back up. But surely it's a hell of a lot better than the personal berating we give ourselves each time we fail in the pursuit of perfect balance. I would prefer some wins, some positive outputs from dedicated focus on something or someone that needs it. And I am learning to try to accept the natural losses that the choice we make may generate. This, for me, is better than a continual sense of failure in every camp that I have pitched a tent in.

Yes, there are days when I roll my eyes at myself at the very calamity of the suggestion that a see-saw could even carry the weight of the plethora of tasks and demands that each day brings. But serving the utmost need of the day and doing that well, rather than trying to do it all and never feeling like you are making the grade, just feels better to me. I am going to try to put away my mental leader board for the game of Me v. The World. Get a bit more comfortable with benching one or two players and changing the game up a bit. The scores will tally themselves eventually. They always do.

CHAPTER FIVE

Guru Doctors

A Prayer to my Doctors

Hail doctors Sandro, Ben, Dan and Eve
Your expertise and love have brought me eternal reprieve
From an insidious cancer, in an insidious place
You all helped extract a nasty tumour attached to my nerves in my face
And I can't forget my herbalist, Dylan Smith, too
Or my Ayurvedic GP in India, Dr Raju
Once the Western team had reached their goal
Your holistic health practices and herbs have kept me whole
Blessed art thou among Gurus,
And blessed is the fruit (my health) of your labours.
Amen

There is not an educator on this planet like that of a life-threatening illness. There is not a time on Earth that you look more desperately to others to save you, not only from your physical or mental injuries but also from your fears, than when an unexpected disease comes your way. And this opening prayer will give you just a teeny-tiny smidge of a sense of the love, adoration and worship I have, and will always have, for the doctors and wellness professionals whom I put my trust in when that happened to me. I have always known that we can and should look to these doctors all that we want or need. And yes, ma'am, they sure as hell do hold in their divine, highly trained brains and hearts so much of what we need to get well. But add to that the power of your own ability to contribute to that healing, the comfort of knowing that you are not entirely on your knees and can heal yourself, and suddenly you feel less helpless, more in control and more focused on what you yourself can do to meet this new challenge. With your own personalised war cry and a glorious sense of capability rather than just intrepid (and natural) fear. Imagine for just a second that with this greater self-reliance and action you could actually influence the health outcome in a positive way.

Sole subservience to doctors and professionals misses the most enormous piece of the pie. A piece that you can not only bake yourself but also humbly eat when you have finished and it all remains intact. This is not about saying that doctors are not Gurus who are unable to remove darkness. A healthy level of deference to, and respect for, their wisdom is undeniably important. They are goddamn superheroes whom I can credit with saving my life. I was helped, and helped enormously. But this is the chapter where I give myself an unapologetic pat on the back for the part in my healing and recovery that I, too, played. Confronting this illness and its severity was *the* moment I truly came to understand that the doctors alone were not going to be enough. That if I truly wanted not just to survive but also remain physically and mentally strong after the trauma had passed, I was going to have to get really intimate with, and harness all of, my own power to add to the force of the strength of those around me and beat this fucker.

And that I did.

Let me try, somehow, to explain my own personal oxymoron and words that I know some people hate being said but that I am going to say anyway. Cancer was ultimately a gift. Not gonna lie, the unwrapping of this gift felt extraordinarily difficult. A lot of impatience while untying the seemingly impossible double knots in the bows that encased it. Painstaking pulls as I ripped off each and every piece of sticky tape that held me back from the joy that was yet to present itself. Multiple rips and slashings as I teared through the layers of paper that were the last thing that stood between me and the positive changes that were about to enter my life once I held that gift in my very own powerful and alchemising hands. Nothing about the way I lived my life has remained the same since I put all that wrapping in the bin.

Accept the diagnosis, not the prognosis

> *I thought things would be one way,*
> *but then they turned out to be another...*
>
> – Everybody –

There are some moments in your life that crystallise with such a solidity in your mind that they never ever dissolve. My cancer diagnosis is one of them. The words of the doctor are like resounding echoes, albeit quieter and more distant now than on the actual day, down the hallways of my heart and mind. "You have a rare and deadly head and neck cancer dangerously situated in the left side of your mouth and face which is attached to nerves and worryingly moving upwards towards your brain. We can operate to remove the tumour and then treat you with radiation, which should give you another five or so years, but then it will likely metastasise to another part of your body and you could die." Exit stage left. That is literally what I did upon hearing these words. My mother, who was there, quickly and involuntarily became my understudy and had to play the role of the star of the show, me, and remain on stage to hear the doctor's remaining lines in the script. In all of the drama, I got stage fright and rushed into the surgery corridors, dragging my co-star husband behind me. I don't think we even talked. I remember the looks of pity from the patients in the waiting room as we passed, my stormy exit into the small office hallway telling an unspoken story of someone who had clearly not received good news. I remember first slumping down against a wall with my knees curled up against my chest, head down, and my arms wrapped around them. My husband hovered over me awkwardly, pacing the narrow space we were in both physically and mentally, understandably not knowing what to say.

Even on a good day, with no bad news, my brain was already like a field of constant rapid-fire. But these two short sentences, uttered so factually by a well-meaning doctor, put my mind into a computerised overdrive as I started to form all sorts of possible algorithms for what I was meant to do with this incoming and new information. From *oh my god, I will not see my one-and-a-half-year-old daughter grow up* to *it's OK, Halan is a good dad, he will take care of her, they will be fine.* From *is this actually happening? It can't be, he has it all wrong* to *yes, you idiot, it is, and you are going to die, your greatest fear has come true, it is over.* And then, after what felt like hours but was truly only minutes, my mental computer completely and utterly crashed. Total system overload. The rainbow wheel of death hovered over my head for a few moments, and then darkness. Nothing.

I don't know whether to explain what happened next as a quick, automated decision or an immediate, deliberate choice. But I stood up. I reached out my hand to my visibly desperately shocked and wide-eyed husband and asked him if we could dance. Anyone who knows my husband knows that dancing is numero uno at the top of his "don't even ask me" list, but he unhesitatingly held me, we got out our imaginary glow sticks, we smiled at each other with tears in our eyes and, smack bang in the middle of a surgery corridor, we danced. Impervious to the curious looks of those around us and momentarily amnesic of my poor mother left behind in the medical pits, we did justice to the infamous proverb and truly danced as if no one was watching.

There was nothing in this moment to celebrate, there was certainly no uplifting music, and I can admit that dancing seems like an odd reaction to the diagnosis. But in those twirls lay my freedom. In those liberating movements, I caught a glimpse of my own ability to make a drab, depressing corridor a more victorious and jubilant space. That dance, even if I didn't know it at the time, was representative of my power to let information be just that, and only that: information. I got to choose, dammit, whether that information was good or bad. I got to choose how I reacted to it.

When something threatens your life in the way this diagnosis did mine, there is no doubt an immediate sense of a spiralling loss of control, a sense of serious victimisation. For me, the window of empowerment in such a seemingly helpless situation was that dance. Regardless of the unchangeable circumstances surrounding me, I still had the freedom to choose my attitude towards them. Some might say I was trying to bury an unavoidable truth, that I was in some form of serious and dangerous denial. But, for me, the only sensible antidote to the trauma was to exercise my freedom and dance in wild abandonment of the prognosis offered up to me. Acceptance of the diagnosis and the somewhat tragic music that came with it? A no brainer. You cannot change facts. But acceptance of a future state that was yet to have occurred or be determined? No way. That part was well and truly within my control. And so began one of the most intense dances of my life.

Ask *what now?* before *why me?*

That doctor may have had some statistical facts and figures in his back pocket and possibly some scientific research to boot, but he did not, and could not, have absolute certainty as to what my future prognosis was. The statistics may indeed have proven, as they reminded me on countless occasions while I silently sang *la la la la la* in my mind to tune them out, that more than 50% of people with my particular cancer have the outcome they were suggesting could possibly be mine. But, to me, on the opposite side of that morbid figure was the entire balance of the total 100 percentage points available where an alternative outcome was *possible*, which was just one giant swimming pool of hope. And so, I dove right in.

The difficult part, however, was that I, too, am not a fortune teller. I also could not teleport myself into a guaranteed happy ending where the cancer was removed, never came back, and my husband, daughter and I lived happily ever after. How, though, could anyone on Earth possibly feel peaceful and in control amidst this strange atmospheric pressure of the total unknown? Even without a death-defying precipice to stand on, the valley of the unknown ahead of you is already terrifying. Pushed closer to the edge by a diagnosis of this nature only made the fear associated with any kind of not knowing even worse.

The blessing of having already learned that nature can serve up terrible experiences for evolutionary purposes that we may come to discover later was nice to have, in the sense that a gift might have been somewhere in delivery transit for me. However, it did nothing for my need to understand on that day how to manage the fear associated with an unknown prognosis let alone the burning curiosity about how I could also influence it to move in a better direction than the one proffered by my diagnosing doctor. I went where every cancer-diagnosed person has gone, straight to *why am I here in this situation? What did I do to deserve this? I am a good person. I do good things. Why, oh why, is this happening to me?*

There are a lot of people who belong to the school of "not even a Mensa member could answer questions like that" and who believe they are questions with zero utility. I think there is, in fact, a valuable place for these kinds of questions but only at the right point in time. I knew that one day I would come to understand the reason this was happening and also find the headspace necessary to face some of the possibly confronting yet useful and educative answers to those questions. But in the midst of a coagulating diagnosis thrombosis, the timing was just not right to ask them.

I needed to hop onto a different starting block. And one that was in the less advantageous outer lane that I seemed to be in at this current moment in time. Instead of asking *why is this the lane that I am in?*, I needed to first ask *what am I going to do about it?* To deviate away from the why momentarily first requires full acceptance of what is. In my earlier years, I used to consider acceptance of *what is* as some kind of defeatist passivity. As if I was somehow demonstrating weakness and capitulating to a bad situation. This idea of just taking what comes, as it does, felt lazy. But now I herald the innate and obvious intelligence in the suggestion. The propeller for positive change doesn't move into motion by ruminating about a past that cannot be changed; it is heavily anchored in the present moment. Accepting what is doesn't mean doing nothing. But from a place of true acceptance, one can circumnavigate the additional suffering that comes with feeling sad over something that you literally cannot control. And this also helps you avoid the loss of precious time that comes with using all of your emotional energy to try to transmute the untransmutable.

The amount of time you spend swimming around in this swamp is directly correlated to the amount of suffering you will experience. Acceptance of unchangeable, already transpired facts is, of course, very different to acceptance of some yet-to-occur hit prediction about the future. The Serenity Prayer, synonymous with helping so many recovering addicts, hits the nail right on its head when it asks God to grant us the serenity to accept the things that we cannot change but the courage to change the things that we can (and the wisdom to know the difference). So, when I got this diagnosis, I moved as quickly as I could to acceptance of the unchangeable fact that I had a very rare and dangerous cancer. But I tried as best I could not to accept as truth any of the future forecasting that had not yet been determined and that I could now proceed to try to change with my own actions. I knew that it would be far more helpful to move swiftly out from under the dark clouds of suffering that come with non-acceptance and non-presence to a place where I would be more capable, more clear and more able to work out what was the smartest thing to do next.

My attempts to move with as much speed as humanly possible towards acceptance were interrupted constantly and would succeed to varying levels depending on whether it was a good or bad day. However, from the day of diagnosis, my commitment to action was as aggressive as the cancer hanging out uninvited in my face. I, of course, stopped work immediately. I then proceeded to read every single book I could find on wellness and self-healing and made sure the array covered multiple and divergent points of view. I did guided mind meditations. I contacted spiritual teachers on Instagram to ask them questions in my search for hope. I forensically researched all the possible ideas, philosophies and teachers that were available, to see what resonated with me.

I remember asking one spiritual teacher the "why me" question well before I was ready to hear the answer. While he didn't say anything even near to it having been my fault, he did ask a single and thought-provoking question: "Is there anything about your life since the cancer diagnosis that remains the same, or have you changed everything?" Without hesitation (or yet understanding the significance of the answer), I said I had changed almost everything. He simply smiled kindly (with no mockery, just knowingness), and that was the end of the conversation. Ouch. But, also, thank you.

It is true, I had begun to totally transform the way that I drank and ate, becoming more and more educated about the eternal truth that diet can be curative medicine. I sought to reduce my toxic load not just from what I put *into* my body but from the products I put *onto* it and those I used around the house. I saw energy healers. I consulted with both Western medical experts and holistic health professionals to understand all the possible options in medicine and in nature that I could use to optimise my health. And I vowed to change my working practices to reduce the stress and toxicity of corporate overload. I left not a stone unturned.

I tried as hard as I could not to do it in an obsessive and possessed manner but more in an excited state of exploration, possibility and discovery. I chose to fill up the cup with positive options rather than read more about the startling possible negative outcomes. No doubt I made the rookie error of consulting Dr Google on many occasions, and as a result of that useless intel I spent countless days and nights in the foetal position contemplating the end that was nigh. Overwhelmingly, though, from all of this education, one thing was clear as day. Many things about my current lifestyle and habits were so obviously unsuitable for optimal health, which was now the slam dunk goal.

When it felt safe and when I felt like I had made solid headway along the paths of both acceptance and then helpful action, I built up the courage to turn the corner and make my way back to Why Me Street. If ventured down at the right time, at an appropriate speed and in a safe vehicle, it can be really empowering to understand how it is that you or your lifestyle and environment may have contributed to whatever situation you are in. And this goes for more than just an unexpected illness. It is equally true in relation to the breakdown of a relationship. Or upon the loss of a coveted job. Asking *why me?* allows you to start to explore and understand what you might want to change in your life to avoid it happening again, but also to uncover if there was, in fact, nothing you could have done differently, to bring you some peace. But having the courage to ask the question – and, believe me, it does require great courage – you might actually be faced with the consideration of why what has happened will ultimately have been a good and necessary thing for progressive change in your life or in the lives of those around you.

With time, I started to see how having this mindset gave me back my own power. Please don't get me wrong, my cancer journey was not a linear peaceful path of spiritual realisation and acceptance. It was a long and windy road full of twists and turns in my mental attitude and physical pain. This experience in my life was the furthest I had ever been from "all roses". But I found some mechanisms that enabled me to cope with and come out of this dark tunnel with some sense of triumph.

I am just so much more comfortable in the zone of personal responsibility than the zone of personal victimisation. I find it much more empowering to feel comfortable saying out loud that some part of the reason for my illness might have come from my own choices. Why? Because this meant that I could change them. I could do something about it. Being rendered choiceless and just accepting myself as plain unlucky felt a lot scarier. How could I really allow myself to continue the delusion that past chain-smoking, all night partying, high levels of unmanaged work stress, no meditation, alcohol overconsumption, bad food and toxic personal and home products had played no possible part at all, when as soon as I was diagnosed, I literally changed every single one of them?

If I am honest, there were so many subtle cues and signs that I was not treating my mind or body as well as I should have been. Post-diagnosis, my husband eerily reminded me of a time when I was smoking after a party and had asked him "What if I get a mouth tumour?" I mean, who asks that? That is inner intuition right there. But I ignored it. How many times did I have to experience the extreme guilt and tortuous physical and emotional discomfort of having to get up early with a young baby after having doused my insides with way too much white wine to try to cope with some of my new mumma-status anxiety the night before? Did I really think that regular full-blown anxiety attacks brought on by incessant, obsessive catastrophising thoughts or work stress were something I should just live with? What did I seriously think my body was feeling when I had polluted it with feelings of anger or resentment about years lost with my mum and sisters?

These things are hard to write down without feelings of shame, even now, but I write them down not to make myself feel bad but to remind myself that the awareness that they were not ideal things was there and that I did not do enough to proactively address them. I have learned the hard way that there is real merit in the strategy of prevention rather than remediation. One happens before the disaster strikes and the other is one big clean-up of mess that has already spilled. And I can tell you from experience, ignoring or not being conscious enough to pick up on some of the signs to make a change can make for one hell of a rubbish removal.

Change can be scary for humans. We don't typically make unprovoked decisions to transform. But waiting or putting it off is a kind of hostility for the present moment. We strangely like to suspend our own action and wait until we are forced, until we have no choice. I can see now that cancer might have been nature's way of forcing me to review what I was doing and understand more clearly that my instincts were right; the way I was living was not the best path to longevity. I couldn't hide anymore from the fact that there were, indeed, many subtle, and even not-so-subtle, signs over the years before the absolute wrecking ball impact of the cancer diagnosis swung my way. But I had ignored them, hesitated too long or lacked the maturity or motivation to remove or change them of my own volition.

Staying put in the status quo and not taking the opportunity to evaluate and change my life at the point in time where the cues to do so were less intense and harmful is an indication that I was not acting as the primary operator of my own life, causing nature to have to move on in, take control of the steering wheel and force the change that was necessary for me to stay here on Earth to keep contributing. Cancer, in one foul swoop, literally removed almost all irrelevancies from my life, enabling me to progress down a more positive and happier path.

The question, looking back, was *did I really need the Universe to shout at me so aggressively, or could I have taken the hint a tad earlier and been in charge of my own evolution more peacefully?* If I had one piece of advice for anyone who has not yet had a petrifying health diagnosis or something equally as threatening happen to them, it would be to know that none of us are immune from it. So don't assume you are safe. And don't wait for upheaval to come with force before you change things that you already know are not good for you. I know now, from lived experience, that if I don't make time for my wellness, I will be forced to make time for my illness. I know which one of those two options I prefer.

Of course, I know that there are also so many life events, traumas and illnesses that can easily be characterised as just unlucky, but in some ways that makes asking the "why me?" question even more important. If you ask that question, though, without a genuine belief that all destruction may ultimately have a purpose, you risk falling into a really unproductive victim mentality and carrying around the heavy feeling that the Universe is working against you. It is quite easy to see how under these circumstances someone may well choose to just wallow in the sheer inequity of it all. Who could blame them?

I have had to examine, since cancer, why I had in the past gotten so doe-eyed in the light of change coming my way or in the way of someone I love. Because, if you think about it, life is always changing. Everything around us is changing as we speak. Even our own physical bodies change at a cellular level minute by minute. Where is Sarah the child? Gone. Where is Sarah the teenager? She's no more. It is inevitable and happening around us all the time. Through this experience, I have learned to try to understand that change does not always have to be so worrisome or problematic and, more so, could actually be the sign of something great that is yet to come, of something you are yet to do and would only do as a result of having undergone this change.

I have heard it said many times before, but life challenges are often the portal to great personal transformation. Through all my studies during and after cancer, I have developed more of a reverence to destruction that may show up in my life, based on a new worldview that it might, indeed, have a purpose. In all my moments of deep thought over this period of my life, I did come to feel supported by the knowledge that, given cancer had not wiped me completely off the face of the earth just yet, it must have meant that I still had relevance here. There must, therefore, still be things I had to do, achieve and contribute.

Just one week after my diagnosis, I went in a somewhat angry and confused state to see my dear kinesiologist. A kinesiologist takes biofeedback from your muscles to identify imbalances that may be causing disease in your body. She told me almost immediately into my session that my body was signalling to her that I needed to give gratitude to my tumour. She suggested that I, through the journey that was to come, should just keep repeating the words "Thank you, tumour, for showing up in my life, but I have learned all the lessons you have come to teach me, and so now it is OK for you to leave." But say it *peacefully* and *with love*. Was she for real? Lost, in that moment, in the haze of my fear and emotions, and looking at her with my then giant tumour-laden face, wondering how on earth she expected me to feel that way, I did not truly appreciate how life-saving these words were going to be.

It reminded me of an analogy used by another of my healers

about the umbilical cord. He had explained that, up to 40 weeks, the umbilical cord is vital to an unborn child's life. However, once born, it is unnecessary and, in fact, dangerous. That does not mean there is now a need to berate or condemn the umbilical cord's ongoing presence. All that you need to say is thank you and goodbye, because, quite frankly, it has shaped your individuality. I only understood the wisdom in these messages after I came to see how much cancer has actually changed me in a positive way and what is has brought to my life. I don't condemn change *as much* anymore. I try now to accept it fully, take action and give gratitude for what it will bring.

I.C.Kangaroos

My husband and I had to move interstate for a surgery to remove the tumour and also for the radiation treatment that was to follow. This meant having to choose to separate from our brand-spanking-new precious baby girl, who stayed at home with my beautiful family for many of the months that we were away. That painful severance from her at such a young age made more of a sting, after the elated highs of her arrival, by the two gruelling years and seven rounds of failed IVF treatments that it took before we could compute (after the fact!) that it had to be her, and only her, making the lengthy and difficult wait worth it.

On the day of my tumour removal surgery, my husband, the brave warrior that he is, waited patiently on his own (and on his birthday) in the hospital waiting room for the nineteen incredibly long hours it took for them to operate. We didn't know, going in, what was going to be the outcome for me physically, and we gave the doctors full permission to do whatever was necessary, without further consultation, to my face and appearance if it meant removing the cancer.

We could cope with what the plastic surgeon had openly said he would try his best to avoid – a visual "train wreck" – if it meant that I no longer had cancer. We were warned that I may lose an eye and suffer some hearing loss. The original plan was open-face surgery, but when the doctors commenced, they realised that they could avoid that if they sought to remove the tumour by accessing it through my mouth. That would require them, however, to literally cut right on out a full half of my upper mouth and teeth. Then use the entire fibula bone in my leg and veins from my feet to reconstruct a new palette and left jaw. As you do.

It is not surprising, then, that post-surgery I was housed in ICU for what was meant to be three days but turned out to be nine. Nine of the longest goddamn days of my life but also some of the most elucidating. I had a tracheotomy, a hole in the front of my neck that reached into the windpipe, kept open so that I could breathe but which robbed me of my ability to speak, like, at all. I was literally rendered voiceless, and for over three weeks. For a verbose and bossy loudmouth, this imposition was one of the toughest aspects, considering what was to come next. In your darkest hours, literally soaking wet in not just everyday fear but deep terror, surrounded by a flurry of urgent and visually chaotic movements and with multiple and constantly different strangers administering procedures and drugs into your own body, to not be able to speak, ask questions, give direction or even object made for a transition in me from an otherwise typically kind, respectful human being into a violent, ferocious caged animal.

This new temporary vocal restriction was made more difficult by virtue of the fact that in ICU you don't lie on a bed. You are perched on what, at best, I would describe as a narrow dentist's chair, and for an inordinately long time. I also had at least eight surgical cords clipped into both sides of my neck, meaning that even the slightest movement was not only not recommended but expressly forbidden. Those cords stayed attached to my neck for many weeks, and as I got more and more conscious, their tugging on my skin and their bountiful heaviness became another drag down into life's potholes. One would think that the mega levels of opioid would help you copioid. But the level of medication they used to attempt the simultaneously impossible and ludicrous task of making any of the above comfortable was like the last ember they added to the virulent fire that was about to erupt in me.

I communicated with my husband exclusively via handwritten notes. You can only imagine how difficult that was to do when you literally cannot move an inch and whilst completely and utterly off your goddamn face on meds. I don't mean just slightly out of it and relaxed. I am asking you to imagine the feeling of being wide awake for nine days straight and completely high on a concoction of hardcore recreational drugs. We are talking about what felt like an induced psychosis but worse: one that you can also consciously recall many parts of afterwards and then, painstakingly, forever.

My husband had the foresight to save every single piece of paper that I wrote on during the entire ICU period and the weeks that followed in recovery. He actually only shared this fact and the notes with me a year later. If I was to bind them all together in chronological order it would read like a mad cross between a children's fairy tale, a psychological thriller, a murderous mystery, a heartbreaking drama series and a biography of a recovered Woodstock drug addict, such was the epic scribing of my anger, fear and hallucinations. I came to instinctively know the time of day my two specialist doctors would arrive, and every time that happened and the hospital doors would swing open, the entire ICU would turn into a 1940s roller rink with handsome waiters skating past carrying mouth-watering cream-topped milkshakes on trays. One day, in anticipation of this mood-lifting delusion, I even penned my plastic surgeon a love letter and hid it in my medical gown, embarrassingly learning, once I came good, the expressions of undying love I had written to him.

I saw kangaroos hop toward me and robots hidden in towels. I complimented nurses for their beautiful tattoos, which they did not even have. Some thoughts were communicated so clearly by my penmanship; others made no sense at all to my husband. Like the one where I wrote that my microphone was levitating like a snake. Or the one where I asked whether my doctors had just told him I could have honey spiders. I still remember crying in frustration for a full day at a nurse not being able to understand that I could, in fact, pay for the surgery of a young boy named Sonny in a cubicle next to me who had no family and who would die without the life-saving treatment that he couldn't afford. Only to learn that both the child and that particularly sad situation were but an imaginary fable in my tortured mind.

In more paranoid illusions, I would ready myself for battle against the evil torturers who I believed were holding me captive in ICU by scribbling desperate accusations and pleas to be saved from this horror to my husband. And I would apparently stab him repeatedly on his chest with the very same pen that wrote these desperate SOS messages when he didn't do what I thought needed to be done if I was ever to get out of there alive. It was not pretty.

I remember being so internally furious at my innocent husband almost the entire time that he stood loyally beside me. Looking back at the notes, and my juvenile handwriting and spelling, I can see why my ill-conceived feelings of hatred reached unnecessary and wholly undeserved proportions. Here I was, thinking I was making myself and my requests abundantly clear. And so when he looked at me utterly perplexed and, worse than that, without taking the protective action I thought I had asked for with such clarity, the level of my feelings of betrayal and contempt increased. As I am sure did his heartbreak. I was convinced that I was being poisoned and kept against my will, with a husband who was in on the evil act. And yet my husband was reading the clumsy words of a three-year-old and sentences that made less sense than the slurred rambles of a wayward drunk.

My heart broke into a thousand pieces when, years later, as I reviewed the pile of my own notes, I found one that my husband had doodled whilst sitting next to me in the ICU. It was a series of stick figures with him, me, our baby girl and our dog all holding hands and smiling – one big happy family. I can imagine he was dreaming for that to be our reality again. I tremor at the confusion and heartache he would have felt as I stabbed his chest with those pens, ordered him to the other side of the curtain and continued to cry alone, creating waterfalls of tears intense enough to hydrate a small community.

And my husband was not the only one to cop it. My nurses, my absolute saviours, deserve the Order of Australia for continuing to focus only on my recovery in the face of the intolerable impatience and distrust I showed them and the disturbing emotional and physical attacks they endured, exhibiting no retaliation other than to shower me with even more unconditional love and care. If you ever want to learn the true meaning of having an attitude of gratitude, then park yourself as a fly on the wall in an ICU of any hospital and watch these selfless angel's work. Then, while you are there, look across to the helpless, scared faces of those who sit lovingly beside the patients in their own world of silent and unimaginable pain and bask in the loving glory of the importance of good old appreciation.

My time in ICU was the closest I had ever come to thinking that death could be a real and imminent possibility. There were some hairy moments while there. I developed a post-surgical internal nasal leak that they were concerned was going into my brain, and to address that further intracranial (open head) surgery was on the cards. During those fleeting moments of returning lucidity between dose injections, I remember feeling so petrified that I might never see my daughter again. And incurable feelings of guilt that I had also momentarily forgotten that I even had her while I fought for my own life. It is true, I was seeing imaginary kangaroos but also simultaneously pondering whether I would ever see anyone else ever again.

One of the most important considerations since ICU that I therefore erected as a permanent archway over the analysis of all future life experiences is whether there is any guarantee that I will see my loved ones later that day. What surely follows such a consideration is a rhetorical question: does that change the way you go about your day? Right? It feels hard and somewhat inauthentic to say I took a whole lot of blessings out of what was seriously the most torturous nine days of my life. But what I can do is name it, without any shame, as one of the most defining moments in my life because as they wheeled me out, bawling my eyes out, all I can remember is making a silent vow that, having been lucky enough to have gotten out of there alive, things were going to have to change. Shit just got real. Big time.

Mind the mind

> *Impossible is just a big word thrown around by small men who find it easier to live in the world they've been given than to explore the power they have to change it. Impossible is not a fact. It's an opinion. Impossible is not a declaration. It's a dare. Impossible is potential. Impossible is temporary. Impossible is nothing.*
>
> – Muhammad Ali –

The number one way to improve my chance of triumph in the face of any kind of difficulty is to have someone tell me that I cannot do it. I treat this less as an insult and more as a challenge to a duel. Add to that my underlying competitive nature, and bingo! Whoever it was that told me that what I wanted to do is impossible, immediately becomes my greatest ally. When the diagnosing doctor didn't look too convinced that there was a high chance of success, it only made me more determined. When others around me, watching how I chose to deal with the news, whispered that I might be in denial, the effort dial turned further clockwise.

There is a tool that we must cherish in our armoury if we are to truly win such battles. And that is our very own minds. I like to think of my mind as a printer. I genuinely believe now that our bodies as they stand on the earth today are direct printouts of the thoughts of yesterday and that our thoughts of today have the immense power to print a new story and outcome for our lives tomorrow. We have all been gifted with a body, but what matters more in determining our fate is how we make use of that precious equipment. Our minds have the power to create our lives, and they certainly have the power to assist our own healing. We need to nurture them, protect them, recognise their untapped capacity and use them as much as we can to positively influence the outcome of our own experiences.

I have never been particularly fond of the statement "I have/had no choice" preceding or following a challenging or disliked situation. Having a choice is the thing that enabled me to cope with being in a tough life-or-death scenario. I prefer to think of life as, in fact, alterable by us; I believe that we can actually change who we are or the situation we are in at any given moment. Undoubtedly, that might not always be easy to do, and, sure as hell, I have used the "I have no choice" card many times (and to my detriment). But I try to kid myself a little less than I did yesterday, because it can be done. Throughout my life, I have come up with many a creative explanation as to why in this or that scenario I really, truly do not have a choice. But looking back, deep down I also knew that I was lying to myself and wish I had exuded more foresight and bravery.

The most confronting set of books I have read on this topic comprises *The Courage to Be Disliked* and *The Courage to Be Happy* by Ichiro Kishimi and Fumitake Koga. I had no choice but to coyly come out of the "I have no choice" cupboard after reading them. Their entire premise is based on the controversial theory of Adlerian psychology, the forefather of which once said that "Meanings are not determined by situations, but we determine ourselves by the meanings we give to situations." Put in layman's terms, Alfred Alder did not believe our past experiences caused our unhappiness but rather that we create conditions like "I am too anxious" or "I am too insecure" precisely to suit our purposes. Because it is easier, feels more secure and way more comfortable to label ourselves in that way.

His view was that we are not victims of our experiences but rather that the meaning we then give them becomes self-determining. Perhaps somewhat ruthless if a person is not ready to accept some level of responsibility for their state of mind, but Alder believed that if you are choosing not to change something about yourself that you know is harming you or holding you back, this is only because you are making the decision not to. The clincher, though, was that Alder did not believe people lacked the *competence* to change but the *courage*. Quite convinced by much of what these books taught, I remember putting them down and thinking that whatever meaning life intended in having given me cancer, that meaning had to be assigned to it by me first. Challenge accepted. Let's make that a good meaning then, shall we?

The most convincing proof for me of the power of our minds to heal our bodies or our lives lies in the scientific concept of the placebo effect. A placebo is a form of medication or procedure prescribed to participants in a study that appears real but that has no active properties or therapeutic benefits. It is scientifically *not possible* that the placebo drug or false procedure could create a positive health outcome on its own. In such research, another cohort of the same study will take the actual medication or procedure, enabling the researchers to understand how effective it is to treat the condition being studied. There is now an abundance of un-ignorable research that has shown that people who have taken a placebo can have not only the same medical outcome but, get this, possibly *even better* medical outcomes than those who have taken the actual medication or procedure intended to treat the condition under review. This suggests that just the *thought* of doing something to make oneself better is enough to actually create that outcome.

This was mind-blowingly exciting to come to learn during a period in my life where the fear of cancer and its recurrence was rife. And when you stop to think about it, it is relevant to so many facets of our lives. Imagine this kind of revelation when a doctor implies the sad outcome is already written on the walls. *You mean I can use the power of my own thoughts to potentially change my biology and influence the outcome of this dire situation? Please, sir, can I have some more?* Bruce H. Lipton's book *The Biology of Belief* and Dr Joe Dispenza's *You Are the Placebo* contain the epic work of two men whom I would describe as spiritual scientists the way they merge the two realms together. Their teachings absolutely rocked my world when I was sick and led the charge that I was starting to make towards the phenomena of taking my healing back into my own hands.

Dr Joe Dispenza, for those who have not discovered his teachings just yet, quite literally was proven to have healed himself from an earth-shattering spinal injury that he was told only surgery and medical intervention could resolve. And he shares openly his experience and the techniques he used to physically reconstruct his spine with no medical intervention whatsoever. Yep, you heard it right, using only the power of his mind. As much as I am a spiritual junkie, I am also a really rational person and can be a tad sceptical at times. Blind faith alone doesn't always quite push me through the door of personal development. Sometimes I need cold, hard evidence. These two authors offered me up an elixir filled with equal parts spirit and science.

The simple truth I took from both Dr Joe's story and his science is that whatever it is that I believe in my mind to be true, is more than likely what will happen. And that what we put our attention on grows. His teachings moved me squarely into an arena of non-negotiability as it related to my need to cultivate a strong mind and become very deliberate about what I was going to believe and focus on moving forward through the medical challenge before me. I wasn't quite enough of a believer (or perhaps lacked the same courage as the author) so as to just ignore the medical recommendations altogether, but I sure as hell wanted to supplement them with greater self-reliance to increase the chances of success.

The placebo effect is clearly rooted in a person's expectations. The more I researched, the more that I started to understand that the placebo operates as a beacon of possibility. The placebo does not make people better – it is devoid of any medical benefit. It is not the pharmaceutical quality of the medication that leads to the physical healing of some of the subjects' bodies. No, it is the pharmacy of positive chemicals that the person creates in their mind with their thoughts of hope, creating elevated feelings of enthusiasm and optimism in their body, which leads to the creation of new cells and improved health.

It's not magic, though. It is not mental voodoo. It requires dedication, persistence and effort. A placebo medication in a scientific context is usually taken over a long period of time and with disciplined daily repetition, meaning that each time a person takes one they are again reminding themselves that they will be better and cumulatively changing their inner state of being. Transformative physical healing and change cannot happen with just one thought. Our minds require the same kind of cultivation and persistent repetitive effort if we want to change the channel and project new programmes into our physiology.

I had already learned from Guru Society about the social indoctrination that affects us from our early years. Scientific estimates are that 40–95% of our behaviour is unconsciously controlled by habits or programs downloaded into our psyche from the moment we are born, precisely by social conditioning. We are talking here about mental programs that have literally been created by someone else, meaning that every single day and with our own thoughts we are unconsciously manifesting life outcomes based on those old beliefs rather than our own inner creativity. It was both alarming and motivating for me to read that such a small percentage of our lives is created with our own conscious minds. So, to know that these teachings and research proved that you can change your body with your own thoughts and emotional state, even about something that was not true now but that you wanted to be in your future, was like the heavens opening and showering me with hope and self-power. This was the bulletproof proof of the mind-body connection that I had been looking for and was going to need to cultivate if I wanted to see my beautiful daughter grow and flourish.

It became clear that I had to stop, as much as I could, thinking thoughts of fear, loathing and death, or my body was going to believe that it was living in that imaginary future reality as if in the present moment. I started to seriously play with the idea that I could begin telling my mind a new story – that I was not afraid and that I was alive, well and perfectly healthy – to send new signals to my brain, every single moment of every single day, to create a new reality and outcome. I could continue to rely on and keep the faith in respect of my doctors' interventions, drugs, surgery and radiation but simultaneously use my own mind to change my inner reactive state in the hope of a better healing outcome too.

A lot of medical experts talk about the inability to change what is genetically determined in our cellular make up at birth, which smashed further into smithereens my sense of self-sufficiency. This was until I found author Bruce H. Lipton, PhD who patched it all back together by teaching me about the scientific study of epigenetics. His passionate view is that that people can, in fact, master their own biology, and it is proven in science that genetically identical cells can have different outcomes as a result of the environment they are exposed to. Could this really be possible? If I was able to change my perception of the world and my circumstances, could I change the chemistry in my body in a positive way? Sure as hell worth a try, right?

At a minimum, I knew that the chemicals I was releasing from my brain mattered. There could be no place in my body for fear and anger, which would only retard my cellular growth and immune strength through the release of unpleasurable chemicals like stress hormones or inflammatory agents. I needed to start, as hard as it felt on many a day, trying to produce chemicals of the nature that are released by feelings of trust, love and joy for optimal biological health. Our genes provide us with a blueprint, no doubt, but our surrounding environment and the way we respond to it has been proven to change and alter our genes. *Mind blown.*

After careful consideration of these theories, I decided to take them on at an unrelenting pace. I used them a lot during my recovery period. The physical pain and side effects from radiation treatment were like nothing I could have ever prepared myself for, and they lasted for an extraordinarily long period of time. I am told that I had the highest dose of radiation humanly possible, every day for six weeks. One of the rarer side effects I experienced from the radiation is a condition called osteoradionecrosis, which, to save you from the medical speak, means that the radiation killed the bone at the same time as it killed the cancer. Quid pro quo? I dunno. But after I returned to work, and was engaging again in constant meetings, calls and conversations, I started to experience an incredibly ulcerated mouth and a really, really banged up tongue. It felt like a very sharp pin or a tiny knife edge deep in the back of my mouth continually slicing up my tongue and causing me immense pain, more enforced silence and an inability to eat any food that was not liquified.

I don't know why, whether it was the hero complex lingering in me or just a burning desire to avoid having yet another associated medical issue, but I endured that pain for way longer than I should have. And it was so far back in my mouth that no one could really see the tiny shard of dead bone that was quite literally forcing its way, with its unforgivingly brittle and sharp edges, through my gums. Of course, after the mammoth reconstruction undertaken and the extreme fragility of my newly constructed face, any kind of extraction or surgery was risky and was too much for me to even bear to contemplate undergoing. It became clear that I was going to have to bring in the battalion of my mind if I was to try and beat this bad boy before that became a necessity.

Perhaps out of fear of the concerned faces from the non-believers, I never told anyone that this kind of mental self-healing was what I was attempting while locked away in my bedroom with my eyes closed and headphones on. But I will never forget the reaction of my dentist as this debrided bone naturally ejected itself from my body with just a gentle tap of her tool after I had placebo-effected the shit out of that sucker in my mind for weeks. I still have the tiny piece of feral bone in a plastic bag, almost as a trophy, to remind myself whenever I need to of my own power. I AM HEALTHY. I AM HEALED. Two phrases that are now as common to my daily affirmations as the sun is to the horizon.

Same shit, different day

> *No matter how long the winter, spring is sure to follow.*
> – English proverb –

The idea that your mindset can mean the difference between healed body and unhealed body, or even just the difference between an ordeal and an adventure, is easy to say, hard to do. But cancer forced me to find ways to put it into practical effect. You will have heard the common saying "same shit, different day", connoting the idea that one's situation is no better or more exciting than it has been in previous days. Another way of saying *here we go again* or of feeling stuck in a Groundhog Day. In certain situations, it can be a little bit the same with my mind.

There are some familiar life scenarios that, no matter how much self-work I have done in respect of mind mastery, I perceive as threatening. No matter the magnitude of the realisation (or the severity of the shame) after I come to learn that my thoughts were actually mind-made, future-based, imaginary creations when the situation resolves itself peacefully, I still find that, faced with that same situation again in the future, I forget all these realisations and the repetitive damaging thoughts take over once more. I am not saying that there exists some kind of infallible mind trickery or that I have a superpower that enables me to ward off all evil from entering my life with a single thought-defying shield. Or that there have been no times where my fearful thoughts and foreboding intuitions have not turned out to be true. As you know, this has already happened to me, but it is rarer than we realise.

In contrast, I could offer up an almost endless plethora of examples of frightening or intimidating situations that I pre-determined the dismal outcome of well before they ended totally contrarily (and quite positively). But all the wasted time, energy, emotion and fear I experienced while locked in my own man-made horror story felt completely justifiable. Funnily enough, it took me a solid three years to write and finish this book, but place me in a situation that scares me and I can write a mental treatise about that situation, including how it is going to tragically end, in a space of mere nanoseconds. I tout myself to be strictly a non-fiction reader and writer. Ironically, not true. 'Cause these mind-made works that I pen in my head are unmistakably, totally and utterly fictional. I literally make them right up. With no facts and with no research. How is it, then, that I struggle to muster the self-belief and confidence necessary to write a non-fiction book about something that has happened to me, yet I can mentally write, self-edit and bring to a damning close a fictional masterpiece in my mind without one iota of self-doubt in its unequivocal perfection and truth?

And it would be negligent, if not just plain rude, not to offer up our good mate Mr Catastrophe a seat at our self-development table. Let's not be mean girls and leave out our frenemy Ms Negativity either. Midway through many a self-deprecating or life-damning conversation, my best friend and I often tell each other to "Stop. You need to *Marisa Peer* the shit right out of that thought." If one of us is stuck in the expression of damaging thought patterns or statements about ourselves or the world that simply are not based on any verifiable rational evidence (and often are totally contrary to already existing evidence of the exact opposite nature), then we draw on our inner Marisa Peer and the author's unique and simple method for quick moments of personal transformation.

I can best demonstrate what it means to *Marisa Peer* your thoughts through example. Instead of *my job is such a drag and I am so hopeless at it,* Marisa would have me roll my eyes and flamboyantly pivot to I *am a highly powered, successful, kick-ass lawyer and am so privileged to work in such glamorous offices and earn such great money and support my family right now without any stress.* When she speaks so contagiously about the need to re-imagine in a more positive way what your negative and pre-conditioned mind thinks to be true, it almost shames me into both becoming aware of and acknowledging the sheer ridiculousness of what it is I am saying about myself or a situation. She challenges me to find another more positive and kinder way of thinking about the exact same thing and repeat it over and over in my mind until it becomes true. Whilst many may call it truth avoidance, I prefer to think of what she teaches as the acceptance and endorsement of the good old "fake it 'til you make it" adage.

Same shit, different page

I refuse to give up on the idea that there is a way out of these kinds of self-inflicted mind mazes. I cannot be aware that I am imposing unnecessary pain on my life without trying to find a way towards improving for next time. So, from all of this medical madness, I have come up with a way to make micro movements in a new direction away from some of these habitual behaviours. A way to help me avoid hiding from the fact that I do these things, often, and eerily well. And that these are not skills I would like to remain on my life's curriculum vitae. I call it *SAME SHIT, DIFFERENT PAGE* (SSDP). I use it in one of two ways and for slightly different purposes. One is used preventatively to help me during or ahead of time, and the other is used retrospectively to allow me to critically assess and adapt for next time. The former is about re-framing and the latter is about re-naming.

The Reframe SSDP

The word *reframe* literally means to "place in a new frame" or to "frame or express (words or a concept or plan) differently". To reframe unhelpful thoughts, fears or anxieties, I will write down on one page the details as I see or feel them in the actual *real-life and current* situation. On the opposite page, I will write about the exact same situation but from a more positive or empowering perspective. Sometimes the facts will be entirely the same on both sides of the page, but there will be a clear and obvious shift in the way that I choose to see or interpret them. A Reframe SSDP sets me up to tackle something that, in my mind, seems impossibly difficult or negative, or to uncover a new and more effective way to manage a problem. The Reframe SSDP is most helpful when I am either stuck in the midst of, or before I have to engage in, a challenging situation.

There is something about writing and reading about the same situation but from two different angles that gives you a less avoidable sense of liberation from the drudgery and an expanded sense of possibility. When short on time and for simpler scenarios, it is also something I can do quickly in my mind. What a Reframe SSDP provides is a display of *the way you tell yourself it is* compared *with the way you could see it if you tried*.

By far one of the toughest situations that would spiral me into a tendency for negative thinking was having to withstand and cope with daily radiation treatments. Every single day for six long weeks the immense physical pain from the severe burns, mouth ulceration and nauseating side effects and fatigue got worse and worse, which was not very motivating to get up and show up day after day. I was told I was having a reaction to radiation on the most severe end of the spectrum. And some would say that I, and my poor, caring family, went into a literal state of shock when we realised that the tremors from the radiation earthquake significantly increase in magnitude *after* it is finished and linger for a totally unacceptably long period of time.

I had to go with progress over perfection with this Reframe SSDP, and there were days where it was straight to hell with any kind of attempt at positive reflection and I blew up balloons for my own pity party with no guilt whatsoever. But to endure the radiation, I found it fantastically helpful to make real efforts to overcome the negative stories about the experience that I naturally gravitated towards in my mind and try, alternatively, to see it in the most positive way possible. You can see what I mean when I talk about a Reframe SSDP for yourself.

From burn to sojourn

> **SAME SHIT**
>
> **(how I tell myself it is)**
>
> The doctors are out of their goddamn minds if they think that I am going to lie down inside of a giant, cold, confined, claustrophobic metal tube every single

day for up to forty excruciatingly long minutes for six entire weeks and have my already incredibly painful reconstructed face and mouth burnt by high-energy zaps of radiation at the highest dose humanly possible. Can they promise me that with each X-ray blaze my high levels of anxiety about the situation will also go up in smoke? Because if they cannot, then I ain't getting in that tube. Nuh-uh. No way, José.

I'm sorry, but did you just say that in order to earn the privilege of sliding into a narrow, enclosed, opaque tunnel, I would first need to have a bespoke plastic mask specially fitted and moulded to within millimetres of my head, face and neck? Why? Why, oh why, would you need such a thing? To ensure I am appropriately locked into place and do not move an inch? Oh, OK then, totally understandable. It's fine, you do your thang, I assume you just want me to breathe, then, using all my magical powers? Mother fuckers. This is all too much. Lie still, Sarah, we are about to pour incredibly warm (aka boiling) melted plastic over your face. It will feel funny (horrendously uncomfortable) but will only take a few minutes (well that is good because asphyxiation is not how I want to leave the planet). Et voilà, a face mask that would make Hannibal Lecter's restraint mask look like a Met Gala fashion statement. Easy. Sure. I will don that every day as you squeeze me into my sausage oven. I won't have any trouble at all breathing, enclosed in a mask and tube that feel narrower than my own windpipe. Hold up, Sarah, check yourself before they wreck yourself, you might have a leftover serve of cancerous tumour post-surgery to eradicate. Be cool. Slide right in and just take a rest, close your eyes and chill for a bit. How hard can it be? Just enjoy the luxurious sounds of silence and meditate. OK, here we go. Clip. Clip. OK, that felt a tad aggressive. What are you doing out there? It is OK, Sarah, we are just locking in your mask to the bed so you cannot move. Eyes roll. Yeah, thanks for keeping me all safe and sound. Bed rolls backwards.

Now I'm immersed in a combative forcefield. A cacophony of militant sounds penetrate my plastic tubular prison. My strategy to rest and meditate can't even go out the window. There are none. It just dies a natural death as quickly as any sense of hope I had that I could manage this. Tears roll down my very still cheeks. The kaleidoscope of noises is rampant and constantly changing. Each instalment of the treatment oscillates between what sounds like jackhammers ripping up concrete, the deep smooth bellows of didgeridoos, the base tremor of techno music thumping in Ibizan nightclubs, a million barbers with their electric shavers skinning heads, terrorists spraying bullets with murderous machine guns, a Sydney summer amplified by a brood of irritating cicadas and, for some reason the most triggering of all, a manic traffic jam filled with road-rage induced simultaneous horns beeping.

Cut to week three. Sound system aversion under control, but now I have to introduce cladding in the form of bad-tasting medical Play-Doh into my mouth to create some buffer space because the multiple, and growing, mouth ulcers and face burns can no longer withstand the pressure of the mask encasing me. To get the sickening nausea taking a scenic holiday inside my stomach under control, long – two-to-three-hour – hospital lie downs and medication become necessary before I brave the chamber.

Getting into the cab each day to get to the hospital is becoming almost unbearable. I start wishing that the MRI tube I once refused to enter would now teleport itself to my apartment. Just so I don't have to take my now emaciated, thin, weak and exhausted body through the crowds at the cafe next to the cab rank and endure the side glances or unabashed stares as people try to work out what a woman in a wheel chair, leg in cast, with half her teeth missing, a tube up her nose and a severely burnt face is doing catching a cab anywhere at all. I shouldn't *have* to do this. I shouldn't *have* to endure this. It is not fair.

Framed as: I *have to* get radiation for my cancer. I am being simultaneously tortured, suffocated and burnt to death, day after day after day.

DIFFERENT PAGE
(how I could see it if I tried)

I can see that the doctors have tossed and turned as much as I have about whether to integrate radiation into my treatment plan. They know and acknowledge up front how hard it will be, but they make it clear that for someone as young as me, with a new baby girl and with such a long life and potential ahead of them, they do not wish to take any chances. Neither do I, so either get on board or go home and give up, Sarah.

They reassure me that they have removed the tumour almost entirely during the surgery, which is miraculous, but explain that they need to ensure a safe margin and can achieve that with radiation. Some people need to have both radiation and chemotherapy, which they do not believe I need, which is great news. And anyway, tube schmube. I have slid through enclosed water slides before and driven multiple times through the Sydney Harbour Tunnel without flicking an eyelid. Hell, back in the day when they were legal, I slid inside a solarium faster than you could say "it's summertime" without any fear. And, let's face it, they were literally coffins. Jim Carrey wore a mask, and he had fun. So can I. Slide me in, sugar.

Oh wow, OK, that's kind of loud and scary. Give yourself a couple of days to feel angry about that, but let's adapt and pivot. If I cannot be in silence, then what else can I do to help the time pass more quickly? I have been listening to and starting to learn about meditation and its benefits. I won't have the headphones or the personal guide lulling me into a state of relaxation and calm, but I have listened to enough guided meditations and know enough about creative visualisation to take myself to another place during those forty-minute periods inside the tube and mask. Close your eyes. Reinterpret the sounds. That is not irritating construction tools, that is Stella excitedly knocking on your door to tell you some good news about her day at school. Yes, they might be the sounds of hardcore beats when you would prefer some Beethoven, but try to remember the incredible fun you had with your friends in your twenties as you danced until the sun came up on a Spanish island. Re-situate those loud cicadas into a future scene where you are poolside, in a floor-length glittering dress, holding your husband's hand as you watch Stella say "I do" to the man of her dreams. And yes, we all agree, tooting horns are not often relaxing, but try instead to visualise a welcome home procession where all your friends are cheering you out of their rooftop windows as you drive down your street after returning home from your long hospital stay, having obliterated your cancer. That will get you through it.

No doubt, the pain and the fatigue are real; it's tough, it's to be expected. Try as hard as you can to focus on other parts of your body that still look intact and feel OK. As for the drudgery of the day-to-day monotony and that reluctance you are naturally feeling about another trip into hospital, how about you try a little sumthin' sumthin', Sarah, and replace all of your *have tos* with *get tos* and see what shifts you can achieve in your perspective here. Go on, give it a bash. How lucky am I that I get to do this? I get to have these treatments that will enable me to live longer. You might be right that it is unfair, but it is necessary and available, and not everyone has the same access to such extraordinary technology. So, hop on in that cab, girlfriend, and you

> will be one ride closer to getting home to your husband and beautiful daughter. You got this.
>
> **Reframed as:** I *get to* have radiation to make me better. I am lying down, taking a sojourn and using this time to reimagine a new future where I am completely healed and lucky enough to have treatment available to enable that to come true.

You kind of see how that works, right? Same story on both sides of the page but just framed up differently and assigned a whole new meaning and experience. And remember that a Reframe SSDP is most useful pre-emptively if you are about to head into a situation you feel anxious or angry about and you want to enter that zone in a good frame of mind. Or sometimes you can also pull it out if you are smack bang in the middle of a pool of negativity or catastrophising and you need it to stop!

There is a wonderful school of philosophical thought which suggests that a situation itself is never good or bad, it is our thinking that makes it so. I have even heard it said that problems are not actually a set of circumstances or a situation but rather a consciousness state. This makes a lot of people really angry because it is as if the blame for what is happening is placed on them. You can see how a Reframe SSDP can really act as evidence for a rather confronting point of view about our personal role in suffering but also, more excitingly, of our ability to remove or change it with our minds.

The Rename SSDP

Alternatively, a Rename SSDP is useful after the fact as a lesson for my future. What I will do is write down on one page a detailed, thought-by-painstaking-thought exposition of every single mental idea or conclusion I had drawn (and why) about a frightening situation, or behaviour of another, that I anticipated (with no verifiable evidence) would happen in the future. On the opposite page, but *only after the situation has already passed and been seen through to an actual conclusion*, I will write the more literal and bare facts about how it actually eventuated, but with none of my own earlier mental narrative. Doing this allows me to rename for next time the situation for what it is and not for what I imagined it to be in my head. It helps me avoid the same wasteful time and energy creating a future fiction in my mind that may never – as this exercise proves – eventuate as I might initially imagine.

Reading the actual, relatively non-dramatic and oftentimes positive, outcome *after the fact*, awkwardly juxtapositioned directly alongside all of the torturous pain I have put myself in with my imagination-fuelled catastrophising, uncovers the both ludicrous and dangerous underbelly of non-presence. It is a useful future reminder, if the crystal ball predictor in me rears her head again, that last time I was in the same situation, I fooled myself into thinking I was a character in an epic award-winning drama when, at best, I was probably a mere understudy in a repeat episode of *Home and Away*. What a Rename SSDP provides is a visual display of *the way you told yourself something would work out* compared with *the way it actually did*.

If I had to pick the most glaringly obvious example of where I struggled, and still struggle a little (but waaaaaaay less than before), to put all I have learned into practice, it would be in the lead up to and during the excruciating waiting periods of the six-monthly MRI scans that I had to have on the path to formal remission (and still do, even after). Simply put, no matter how calm, no matter how at peace, no matter how healthy or confident I had been right up until this precarious date, these scans, quite literally, scared the living shit out of me. And yet, thankfully, they never turned out the way I had told (and unnecessarily tortured) myself they would. See for yourself what I mean when I talk about a Rename SSDP.

You big fat scanny cat

SAME SHIT

(the way I told myself it would work out)

As if out of nowhere, I start to feel a numbness on the left side of my upper lip. It feels as if a giant bee has stung me or I have just completed major dental surgery and the anaesthesia is still wearing off. Work conferences and conversations are hard work on my heavy mouth. As I touch around my face to assess the breadth of the perimeter of the numb region, I come to my left eye. As I rub the inner corner, I hear a squeaking sound as if an old, haunted door is creaking or a rubber ducky who has seen better days is being squeezed. Not good. When I originally was diagnosed with cancer, each time I touched my face I felt pain. OK, this isn't pain per se but it's an unusual sound and sensation and could mean a new cancer is pushing down on my nerves. I forensically examine my face close up in a mirror. Shit. Fuck. What is that tiny white pimple on the border of my left pupil. Like what the actual fuck is that? That's it. For sure. I have a cancer of the eye. Yup. That has to be what it is.

Frantic call to doctor. Doctor requests that I do my usual six-monthly scan now, a few weeks ahead of schedule. Why? Why would he ask me to do that? He would only ask me to do that if he was worried about cancer recurrence. Otherwise, he would just wait until my next scan. God damn it, why did I even tell him? Holy shit. What if it really is back? How would I tell Stella? Oh. My. Goodness. I will never see Stella grow up after all. Bawl my eyes out for a good hour whilst also trying breathing techniques as I madly pace the house like a tortured detective trying to solve a murder mystery. Major, unrelenting panic attack sets in. Call Mum – bawl. Hang up mid-sentence. Go find husband. Scream at him that he doesn't understand the fear. Slam every single door in the house. OK, OK, c'mon, Sarah, you got this. You have done millions of scans with positive outcomes. Nope, have not got this at all. Write frantic email to doctor and ask him why he wants a scan. Informed it was a "mere precautionary measure" and encouraged to "be calm". Calm? Is he insane? I have cancer recurrence! I am going to die! YOU BE CALM, YOU ASSHOLE! Feel bad for calling my hero an asshole. Oh well, he will understand.

Attend scan. Same nurse I always have greets me knowingly and can sense my nerves. She reminds me her name is Astra (for real). I tell her my name is Zeneca and we laugh, which momentarily diffuses my anxiety. Head mask locked on, slide into suffocating narrow tube for close to one hour. Meditate my way through the scan and all the verbal directions not to move an inch or we will have to start again. Nailed that. Sit up from the scan and immediately start a scan of my very own – studying with X-ray vision both radiologists for any sign at all on their faces or in their body language that they saw something concerning. Are they being nice because it all went well or are they being cheery because they feel sorry for me? Can't tell. Don't ask, Sarah, just keeping scanning. Nurse seems genuinely relaxed and gleeful. As I leave, she says, "I will see you again in six months." Bingo. Jackpot. Boom Town. She wouldn't say that if she saw something cancerous. Phew. Business as usual.

Take a few steps out to the front reception to settle up. Feeling pretty calm now. As I go to pay the $500 fee, one of the receptionists leans over and says to the other, "Given the circumstances, we will bulk bill her on this occasion." The other nurse looks slightly taken aback, as if that has never happened before. Panic sets back in. What fucking circumstances? I always pay $500. Why don't I have to pay this time? Do you know something I don't know? Is it because you know that the scans showed I have cancer again? Please, just let me pay the $500. I don't need any special discounts. I am super healthy and am not a victim. Get bulk-billed and leave, gutted.

Three days (including a weekend) uncomfortably

wedged between the scan day and the results day. Planned own funeral. Made decision I want people to dance to Janet Jackson's "Together Again" after the service. Hassle husband all weekend for drinking too much wine and reducing his longevity given he will be a single parent soon and I need him to live longer for Stella. Phone rings on Monday. Deep inward breath suctioned in tighter than a vacuum cleaner, tortured wincing face, hands firmly positioned under bum. GP gives me an instant thumbs up, scans are all clear. You could have generated electricity for a small community such was the wind force of my outward breath.

Named as: Cancer is back. Panic attack. I will die soon.

DIFFERENT PAGE
(the way it actually worked out)

After six months of relatively no issues with my face and living a really normal, positive, healthy life with my family, I become aware of a heavy numbness in my face during a period of significant work stress and a strange, very slight squeaking noise in my left eye when I rub it. I have actually felt both of these symptoms many times before along my journey, but, in the panic, I have forgotten completely. My doctor and my family remind me that last time I experienced numbness in the face was also during a period of high work stress and exhaustion, but that sensible correlation is also ignored in my state of panic. Total tune out to the voice of my caring, wise mother who reminds me that doctors had openly informed me before they even operated that my life would be scattered with side effects that impacted the comfort of my face and mouth and that this was to be expected.

My scans are already due to take place this month, so I would have been getting them done in next few weeks anyway. Beautiful, kind, ever-present doctors explain that it would be negligent to not use scans to rule out all possible consequences and reiterate that I would be having them at my routine six-monthly check-up anyway. This kind of practical and sophisticated logic is just unable to be computed by my catastrophising and ancient Commodore 64 desktop brain. Doctors also admit that they ask me for scans because they know that I will painfully self-diagnose if they don't rule it out scientifically for me. Ouch. That hurts.

Meteoric measures of stress imposed upon my nervous system for something that has not yet happened. Days, literally entire 24-hour days, of my precious life and the lives of those around me squandered. Poof. Gone. Up in smoke. Mum, husband, daughter all drawn into the deep, dark waters of the panic pool to help me stay afloat.

Radiology nurses are not even legally permitted to say anything to a patient before the radiologist has had an opportunity to review the scans and compare them to your prior ones, so their silence is absolutely meaningless. There is literally zero practical possibility of the receptionist having been briefed on the outcome of my

> scans by these nurses within the fleeting three seconds it took for me to walk the two metres between the scan room and the front desk. The receptionist is obviously referring to the circumstances the entire community is in during a period of COVID-19 lockdown and is being kind. News flash, Sarah: It Is Not All About You! Also, you ungrateful sod, you just saved five hundred precious bucks.
>
> The tiny white pimple on my eyeball is a pterygium, which is effectively a sunspot, and the treatment plan is to "wear sunglasses more". The squeaky eye is an air pocket as a result of my mammoth prior facial reconstruction and is nothing to worry about. And we already know that the scans showed absolutely no cancer recurrence at all. In fact, the numbness could actually be a sign of nerve regeneration and healing – the irony of that is not lost on me.
>
> **Renamed as:** Got a scan. Results were all clear. Worry was fruitless.

Now when I go for scans, I still get nervous but I literally recall this Rename SSDP to reduce the veracity of the fear and as a reminder that chances are everything is going to be A-OK.

CHAPTER SIX

Guru Beauty

Beauty is a short-lived tyranny.

– Socrates –

Beauty is the beast

The funny thing is that when you are told you have a giant tumour attached to nerves inside of your face, one which you can actually see when you open your mouth wide enough, your level of rapid and unequivocal acceptance for whatever is required to be done to your outward appearance to get that thing right on out of there is stratospherically high. But after it is successfully removed and you re-enter everyday life, your sense of ecstasy for having survived at all does, unfortunately, start to wear off. So, the loss of half of your upper row of teeth, a very sunken left eyelid, the obliteration of one nostril to the point of non-functioning and becoming mostly deaf in one ear all start to emerge as yet another set of challenges to overcome.

In some ways, I was lucky. I have never really considered myself as having the kind of attractiveness level that enabled me to rely on it for my own sense of fulfilment. And so, beauty is not a Guru that I personally had given away much of my power to, growing up. While I was never one to look in the mirror and completely recoil, I certainly never clocked my own reflection and thought *god damn, girl, you are banging!* either. In the period of my life just before cancer and the associated surgery, I had taken, at most, a very basic sort of contentment in the way that I looked.

In high school, where we know the pressure to fit in is at its peak, I was known to wear my UGG boots and my Guns N' Roses ripped T-shirt to casual days without one skerrick of care about what that might mean for my popularity status. I had braces for most of my senior years, pimples to give Mount Vesuvius a run for its lava, and the frizz in my thick-as-hell hair at the slight sniff of humidity was not pretty. As I grew into my older night-clubbing party-girl years, I definitely sought to elevate my good-looking game. Probably more Victoria's Basement than Victoria's Secret vibes in this particular part of my life, but I did give the "I'm not second-hand but my clothes are" vintage look a red-hot crack while it was cool.

It really was not until my early thirties, when I lived in Geneva and then Paris for several years for one of my corporate legal jobs, that my ego came out to play with its good mate beauty. This temporary phase that reared its head was less about how I looked physically and more about my new obsession with "labels". It was as if an entirely new belief system emerged that "anyone who's anyone" is wearing *this* shoe or *that* bag and therefore so must I. Or I shall perish into irrelevance or die. Dramatique! I can tell you that I came home from Paris dripping in couture and feeling fashionably mature but having bid, for the moment, my self-sovereignty adieu. It was one of the first times in my life where I believed that what I was worth had a genuine connection to the fashion house I had gifted with three thousand dollars to sell me what was essentially a piece of leather with a metal badge on it that everyone else was wearing. I*'d be nothing, nothing, nothiiiiing* (yes, I am serenading you, my extortionate YSL bag), *if I didn't have youuuuuuuu.*

The one consistent theme through all of these different stages of development in my relationship with how I looked on the outside was (and still is) my flat-out refusal to interact with, feign interest in or try to work out how to apply it. Makeup. I have always had a very strange and defiant aversion to "lippie" and always felt that I looked "cheap" in it. I look now in wonderment (and maybe some concern) at my eight-year-old daughter who at times appears to need me to put her nappy back on as she walks into a MECCA makeup store, such is the level of "I am going to pee my pants" excitement in her already beautiful face and body.

The concern probably comes from my awareness of the current state of the world as it relates to the constant barrage of messaging, social media pressure and manipulative advertisements. About beauty products that will perform a whole round of non-surgical transformations or improvements on what probably doesn't need any work at all. About garments and accessories that will bring a new cachet and social status for the lucky few who can afford them. All of which are generated to invoke a sense of "lack", with the unabashed goal to ignite a desperate feeling of "want" or, worse, the more nefarious belief that you truly do "need" something to make you more beautiful.

Until my physical looks were so dramatically changed by my surgery, and on the one part of my body that, unless I wanted to pursue a new career as a balaclava-wearing bank robber, was never able to be "covered up", I had never really had any reason to deeply consider what I would do if the damage to my face couldn't be corrected. Until then, I had always been happy enough with my looks and never really relied on them as any kind of lifesaver. I was content to lean more on my personality to accompany me towards the places that I wanted to go.

Dependence on beauty for self-love has not been a hugely prevalent issue for me. But I could, in parts of myself at certain points in my life and based on all the glaring mental health impacts that reliance on beauty can place on vulnerable people in modern society, see the more severe fragility that could be created if one was to consider their self-worth appendaged to the ongoing maintenance of that outward appearance.

I couldn't help but start to wonder... certain as the sun, rising in the east, if we lived our entire lifetime with happiness dependant on staying in our prime, could beauty become the beast?

The hard tooth

It is true that extreme vanity or obsession with looks has never been my wheelhouse, but when you get in the ring with cancer and come out with no teeth, you are forced to face the hard truth of the infamous proverb that it is what's on the inside that really counts. Easy to say that a pleasing physical appearance is not a guide to character when you have one that is relatively appealing. But absolutely necessary to understand and live by when aspects of that beauty are taken away from you. Never have I ever been more astutely aware or convinced, as parts of my own were impacted by my surgery, of the danger of relying on your external appearance for your sense of self-worth.

I honestly don't think I would have stepped outside my house for many years after my cancer surgery and radiation if a reliance on beauty had ever had a strong hold on me. Especially given the surgical impact was to the part of my body that is my direct and first interface with all other beings in this world, all day and every place I go. And the fact that my mouth is one of my most used (and often overused) body parts, critical to what I get to eat, how long and how easily I can talk to people without pain and, most impactfully, what I had once used to passionately kiss my partner with. There is nothing wrong at all with wanting to look good. I am definitely not saying that. But if I had lived a life in reliance on my looks and only my looks for my personal happiness, Boy George, would I have been in mega trouble after this surgery.

It is our ego that attaches its worth to and identifies with our physical form rather than our inner essence. We all know that sinking feeling you get, or that dip in your mood that can arise, if someone criticises your appearance in any way or doesn't validate your own opinion that your new haircut or outfit looks good. Ideally, the opinion of the other should not even rate on the self-esteem tally card, but we all know that it does, and it is critical that we learn how to continually try to move further and further away from that kind of impact.

Whenever I would encourage people in my life to talk openly to me about the impact to my face and not be afraid to ask questions rather than quietly wonder, two of the most common enquiries people had were how do I still manage to go into a formal and corporate workplace with the same confidence and whether it had impacted my marriage or intimacy now that I looked slightly different.

I don't think they were asking me because they thought I looked hideous and couldn't believe I could ever feel comfortable. I felt the questions came more from the angle of fascination and maybe also because they were pondering whether they could do it themselves, given how much appearances do tend to matter to people. People were genuinely awestruck that I seemed to be doing it without too much worry. Well, at least from where they were standing.

If you consider the hard tooth of the matter, from the second we enter the world, our physical appearance changes enormously and naturally year on year on year. In direct opposition to this, we are bombarded at full force with advertiser and influencer megaphones preaching to us that this change – ageing – should be avoided at all costs. Is it any wonder that people fall apart if they feel they have completely failed at what is essentially an impossible bypass?

From seeing the funny side to feeling pride

Make no mistake about it, since the surgery my once preciously natural confidence about my appearance can, on bad days, melt like ice in the hot sun, and I am often found trying to anxiously mop it up off the floor. But without making a total mockery of myself (or anyone that might feel or be disfigured in any way), I did initially try to use humour as one antidote to any negative vibes as they started to creep in. Laughter really can sometimes be the best medicine. I think it's actually been proven somewhere that one minute of anger weakens your immune system for 4–5 hours, whereas one minute of laughter boosts your immune system for over 24 hours. If I was ever wallowing too deep in my own self-pity, it was not uncommon for my family to send me texts with GIFs that used my post-surgery horror photos superimposed on a faux Vogue cover.

The complicated and highly uncomfortable nasal tube I'd had installed post-surgery was there for quite a long time after I got home. Whatever they had moved around inside my facial anatomy during the surgery had meant that sometimes the food and drink ingested by my mouth would feel a tad disoriented and, instead of making its way safely down my throat and into my belly, go upwards and then, gleefully, and often with zero warning, mistake that plastic nasal tube as a slippery dip and come whooshing out of my nose. Even after the tube was removed, this continued to happen out one of my nostrils and still does to this day.

Instead of suffering the embarrassment of such a strange and unexpected facial mechanism each time the coffee would spurt out during a boardroom meeting or the red wine would spill out at the dinner table, I would, of course, wince ever so slightly. But, more so, I would try to laugh (and hope that the other person would laugh with me, not at me). My nephews started asking me to do it at family events like a party trick, and my husband even once went to catch the red wine spurting out of my nose into his own cup to avoid any wastage!

My plastic surgeon used a skin graft from my calf to replace my mouth palette, meaning that part of my leg was literally now in my mouth. Add to that the fact that I was not permitted to shave my legs before surgery to avoid infection risk and you don't need to be a mathematician to put two and two together and understand that post-surgery, and to the day that I type these words, my leg hairs continue to grow in my mouth. Yep. You read that right. But instead of constantly crying over such a gross (and irritating) monstrosity, I would cheekily berate my radiation oncologist for having done a totally crap job. I lost a whole host of the hairs on my head from radiation, he could have at least done me the courtesy of lasering those leg hairs right on out of my mouth. Useless!

With time and as I allowed myself to truly contemplate these physical changes and accept their possible permanency, it got me thinking about how I could reframe this part of my experience. My daughter, Stella, for example, said that I should be thrilled because the tooth fairy was going to make me one rich lady with such a bulk donation to her treasure chest. But in all seriousness, with more time and space between the trauma and the outcome, I started to realise that I am not Robinson Crusoe here. There are so many people in this world who have lost a limb or the normal function of a part or parts of their body. There was no need for me to try to deflect the loss of my teeth with humour anymore.

With that came a greener shoot in the form of looking at the changes to my face with more of a sense of pride about what I had achieved and overcome. Instead of seeing the gaping hole in my smile as some kind of loss and misery, I started to try to see it rather as a badge of honour.

Boy, do I have work to do to truly rooly accept this loss, especially as it relates to my worry (totally unnecessary, he tells me) about how my husband sees me. When I look now at photographs taken one week before I even knew there was a tumour in my face, so innocently unaware of what was about to happen, it is a good reminder of how fleeting having these physical features or positive emotions about them can be and, more so, how quickly they can be taken away from you.

Those pre-cancer pictures of me with my husband and daughter so joyful and blissfully unaware, ignorant in that moment of what was around the corner, are important reminders for me to enjoy all present moments. And to stop relying on anything I have that can and will change as my source of happiness. The journey of acceptance is a continual process with many ups and downs. But I find that it does feel better for me (and I imagine for everyone around me) to completely own my new look simply as who I am with absolutely no apology for it and no attempt to cover it up. So, I openly laugh, I try not to cover up my mouth with my hand nervously when

I speak and I smile widely as often as I can. As that became my authentic modus operandi, I found that people started to notice it far less.

Ironically, when I was a child, I was born with a gap between my two front teeth that could fit two 50-cent coins between it, to give you a sense of its largesse. I was teased often as a kid with school yard songs like *"Gappy's unhappy cause she wet her nappy"*. What did I do the second I was able to? I got braces to close that gap up that I was born with – and then lost them all anyway! Great spiritual Gurus, if asked the question, will openly tell you that the reason they do not cut their long beards is out of respect for their God-given form. The question from the Guru's point of view is rather *why do men remove them?*

We do, no doubt, live in a world where surgical and medically supported enhancements and injections to our faces and bodies are more and more common and the societal pressure to avoid ageing starts so early. Any kind of identification with our external appearance as being who we are can mean that we suffer when our physical form starts to age or deteriorate in any way. I am not saying it's not OK to wear makeup, take pride in our appearance and buy nice clothes. But my aspiration after having my appearance altered in such an impactful way is now to try rather to enjoy those things, for sure, but never to wrap my identity and happiness up in them so much so that I would unravel if, god forbid, they ever changed. Which they absolutely will.

This whole life experience really caused me to ask myself *can I simply love what I have been left with post-surgery?* Or, more generally, *can I love whatever is natural about my appearance?* My daughter has the same natural gap between her teeth that

I had when I was young; I hope she never seeks to alter it. Perhaps she will look to her mumma and not place as much emphasis on having teeth anyway! #accidentalrolemodel

CHAPTER SEVEN

Guru Spiritual Leader

The best teachers are those who show you where to look but don't tell you what to see.

– Alexandra K. Trenfor –

After surviving the surgery and radiation, which did successfully remove every bit of the cancer (yay!), I will admit to becoming a tad one-eyed about building a very sturdy drawbridge between myself and the threat of metastasised recurring cancer. Between myself and my own fears about it ever coming back. One that I could hoist and lock permanently closed, never to exit the safe citadel of No More Cancer.

This analogy of wanting to bolt myself inside such a blockhouse, never to take the risk of leaving and exposing myself to new experiences, foods, products, people (or anything, quite frankly) that could be the reason that the cancer would creep back into my body is actually not an exaggeration. The same way a drawn drawbridge is intended to prevent attacks from the enemy, I, too, wanted to create and retreat into an impenetrably secure harbour to shelter my recovered self from the return of anything that could threaten its welfare. All the doctors had to do was tell me that metastasised cancer cannot be cured (yet) and the percentage chance of that happening to me (can't remember, tuned out), and so began the immediate and urgent construction of my very own fortress. Filled with all kinds of armoury that I could adorn to protect me as best as possible from any returning foe moving forward.

I think the analogy appropriately communicates the fear (and determination) that comes with never wanting to be ambushed by something this difficult again. However, perhaps less obvious is that employing such a solid defence strategy also comes with a serious sense of isolation, a feeling that you are now trapped alone inside a place that is just too risky to leave. Left with no choice but to completely alter your life if you truly want to maximise the likelihood of longevity – what you eat and drink, what products you apply to your body, how you spend your days, what job you choose to do, how you manage and respond to stressors – can absolutely leave you feeling like a lone captive with the pressure of a whole lot of new decisions to make.

It feels as if no one else around you has to, wants to, or is as motivated as you are to do the same because they don't have that same looming fear hovering over their heads. Fair enough. But I would often say to my husband as I watched him hoover down a non-organic greasy burger and fries or sip his second glass of red wine that he needed to understand: I wish like hell I could do that too without any guilt, but I don't have that option if I want to maximise my chances of survival.

Or I would enviously watch him as he went freely about his day doing whatever pleased him and his senses without worrying about whether he had done his breathwork and meditated because he didn't see them as necessary priorities in order to live a long life. Even something as simple as seeing him douse himself in luxurious fragranced shower products with no concern because he wasn't on the same mission to reduce the toxic load in his body to avoid cancer recurrence would rattle me.

There were days when I am sure he thought I had gone mad,

and there were also days when I just longed for him to come and sit with me all safe and sound from any foreign invasions in my new protective fortress and stop playing about in those dangerous territories on the other side of the wall. At best we had intermittent dips together in the surrounding moat, but, if I am honest, for a long time after my recovery I felt like the responsibility to survive dominated my consciousness and the responsibility to rescue and nurture me dominated his in a way that caused momentary emotional separation between the two of us. Not to fear, we did find our way back out into the free and less afraid paddocks of love, togetherness and moderation, but that required me to go deep in a way I am about to share.

Let's Get Spiritual

There was a period post-cancer removal that I can live with being told I was a tad selfish, obsessive and chaotic about my mission to try and learn about any possible fad, craze, diet, treatment or healing if there appeared to be reasonable logic behind its utility in keeping cancer at bay. In many ways that change in me has been lasting. I remember reading a wonderful book by Dr Kelly A. Turner called *Radical Remission: Surviving Cancer Against All Odds* about her in-depth study of the approaches and strategies employed by hundreds of cancer patients globally who had experienced radical (or unexpected) remission, but specifically those people who had done so without conventional medicine or when such medicinal approaches had been tried but failed.

She shared the summation of that study, which included the top nine consistent themes that she believes helped turn these terminal patients around. What I found captivating about her research was how many of those factors related to the person's ability to heal their own body and were within in the physical, emotional and spiritual arena. The book motivated me further to not sit passively and wait for a miracle but rather to be an active participant in my own prevention strategy and proactively choose the right changes to make to my life to give myself the best chance of remission too.

Some of the common findings about people's behaviours and activities who went into remission following a terminal cancer diagnosis related to taking control, following intuition, being positive and releasing old emotions. I already understood the utility of many of these ideas, and so I continued my efforts to improve in all of these areas. I also had incredible social support within my friends, family and community networks, which Dr Turner found was another one of the critical factors in the studied patients' survival stories. Community and family had always been a part of my life that I had never been shy to lean on. And I had just given birth to the biggest reason for living that I could ever hope to muster. But my fascination was piqued by her very clear direction about the importance of diet, the use of holistic herbs and, perhaps the least known to me at the time, the deepening of a spiritual connection.

I believe it is all about keeping an open mind and finding the approach that feels most resonant for you. After a lot of trial and error in the diet space and following through with at least a pilot test of every single spiritual healing technique or provider that someone would recommend, nothing felt as right as when I serendipitously had one single approach land on my lap as neatly as a meal on a stable table and that also tasted really yummy. And one that provided me with a solution that covered so many facets of Dr Turner's recommendations. My younger sister had randomly told me about a podcast called *Vedic Worldview* by Thom Knoles, who is a great master of the meditation technique that I had already learned and had started to make a discipline in my life.

The very next day, after she told me about him, I got an email from a friend who I had not heard from for a long period of time inviting me, somewhat out of the blue, to a workshop run by the same spiritual teacher, who happened to be visiting here in Sydney in the coming weeks. The Universe was clearly sending me a message, so I enrolled in one of his talks and started listening avidly to his podcast. And so began my journey towards a Guru Spiritual Leader who offered me the path I had been looking for in order to step up my healing journey on both a physical and an emotional level.

I don't know about you, but I have enthusiastically dived into many super well meaning, awe-inspiring self-help books and eagerly attended many wellness courses and retreats and each time had begun with the same primary goal: to feel better about myself. Yet sometimes as I read that last crucial line or said goodbye to the last equally desperately seeking student, I actually felt as if my (admittedly self-imposed) failures were truer than ever before and therefore that the self-work had stalled me. I was also left wondering how on earth I would continue on each new path without the Guru I had found and their wisdom by my side, counselling me every step of the way. And so, often, the walk of shame back to base and back to seeking new or different answers "out there" and from someone else would recommence again and again in an ever-repeating loop.

I have seen (and it's so common on social media) that experiencing any kind of trauma commonly leads people towards Gurus of some nature who promise to assist you with healing. Their teachings and wisdom are incredibly important, but what always niggled in the back of my mind was whether it made good sense to get hooked on that particular person or teaching in any kind of cult-like fashion. So much so that you create a new dependency, and then, when you leave the course or put down the book, you are still in the same spiritual mess and so need to look back continuously to that Guru for an ongoing ability to cope and be happy.

As a relatively non-religious human being, this was the first period in my life where I started to see the benefits of a spirituality-based approach to understanding life. The more my new Guru Spiritual Leader (and his current students whom I came to meet within the community) taught me, the higher the vibrational resonance between what he was teaching and how I had already started to see life, merging into a more complete and clearer picture. Considering the level of benefits and transformation this particular Guru brought to my life, I got very close to backtracking towards believing that reliance on an external remover of internal darkness was, perhaps, not such a bad thing after all. But Thom and his teachings would never have supported that. He led me on a path towards my own self-sufficiency without me even realising it until I experienced the bliss of living that way for myself.

This newly discovered Guru provided me with the foundational knowledge to explain my own worldview, helped me find answers to so many open questions that I had been wanting to resolve my whole life and led me to a new sense of who I am and what I am capable of. But what enamoured me the most was that his key lesson was one I would get zero out of ten for if I was to develop any kind of over-reliance on him or the scriptures underpinning his teachings: self-sufficiency is, in fact, the very aim of his teaching's game.

Thom invited his students to experiment with what he taught, to treat it all as one hypothesis and not to act on it as a matter of blind faith but rather to conduct our own research. And so began a period rippled with both great emotional turmoil and challenge but ultimately great clarity. A phase in my life of less *uh-ohs* and more *a-has*. The dropping of multiple mental pennies and the laying of the last stepping stone I needed to cross the river towards discovering my new best mate: *Youru*.

WTV?

Look out, WTF, there is a new acronym in town. *What the Veda?* You would be forgiven for experiencing the sensation of bewilderment that is bound to accompany this turn of phrase. I certainly felt that way when Thom started to teach me what these magical mystical Vedas were. I am still deep in the throes of learning, but these ancient bodies of wisdom have shone illuminating light for me on what it is we are really here for. The Vedas provided me with a lot more of a rock-solid basis upon which to continue my climb towards greater self-sovereignty, but this time with the belief that such a light at the end of a very-dependent-on-others tunnel is actually possible.

My Guru Spiritual Leader did forewarn, as I embarked on a variety of hugely instructive and enlightening knowledge courses and lectures about the Vedas spanning a period of over three years, that there is an important purity in the teachings of the ancient scriptures which can be inappropriately disturbed if they are shared out of full context or explained by someone who doesn't necessarily have the experience to do so properly. For that reason, but also because I truly believe that one's own personal exploration and study of the spiritual concepts taught in the Vedas is, by far, the most effective way to transfer the knowledge, I will just share a small part of what I personally have taken from the teachings.

At the very least, what I do want people to know about is the very existence of the Vedas, as I get a lot of half-cocked heads bearing confused faces when I tell people that I study them. And I do want fulfilment seekers to explore them further if some of the core concepts and blessings I have taken from them resonate. The Vedas embedded within me a spine-tingling level of excitement by teaching me that the boss lady of all of this chaos, the person with the highest degree of influence and control over what happened next, was me (and always had been). That I was, in fact, already all of the things I had been searching for *out there*. Peaceful. Joyful. Fulfilled. But let's start at the very beginning, shall we?

The word *Veda* in Sanskrit simply means "the Knowledge". The Vedas are a large body of texts which originated in ancient India. The Vedas are said to be *what is heard*, meaning that they are revelations of sacred sounds heard by ancient sages through divine inspiration after intense meditation and passed down through generations between parent and child or teacher and student. They are made up of knowledge which has been orally transmitted since as early as c.1500–1200 BCE. There is also a large body of epic Vedic literature which represents what is remembered (rather than heard) and that contains Vedic philosophy and knowledge, which has also been instructive to me. Books such as the *Bhagavad Gita*, the *Ramayana* and the *Mahābhārata*, to name a few. I learned most of what I know about the Vedas, however, through a series of recorded lectures called *Exploring the Veda* delivered by Thom Knoles many years ago and taught now by current Vedic meditation teachers who have learned under his instruction.

I grew up a non-practising Catholic Christian, and, for whatever reason, religion never really interested me at all. Then the older I grew the more it seemed to me that religion had the capacity to be used as the basis for explaining away what felt like very hateful, destructive and separating behaviour. Many of the teachings learned at school felt very archaic and sometimes I would find myself wondering whether religion had failed to keep up with the Kardashians and adapt in ways that were more relevant to the modern world.

The younger, more rebellious anti-authoritarian in me also took issue with being given a set of commandments and told that if I followed them, I could find God. It left me with a youthfully immature and very uneducated perception that God was snobby and exclusive and would only let you into da club if you had learnt a set of house rules and stuck to them. Despite some of the important values underpinning many religious faiths, God always felt too elusive for my liking. But I did like the idea of there being some kind of higher power that I could look to for answers in times when I needed guidance.

It has been said by some that the Vedas are owned by the religion of Hinduism, but that is not how it has been taught to me. My understanding, rather, is that the Vedas are not religious texts as much as they are bodies of wisdom and that they are not owned or authored by the Hindus (or, in fact, anyone) but rather owned by the world. The Vedas may be deeply applied and revered in India, but their philosophies are universal in their application and the knowledge is equally relevant to all countries, cultures and religious backgrounds.

This kind of inclusiveness seemed much more like my schtick. The Vedas teach what is really the truth of life for all of humanity. I know everybody says to never read the last page of the book before you start, but it is easiest for this Vedic student debutante to begin with where the Vedas end – if any of my learnings shared are to make good sense. The central concern of the last part of the Vedas is the connection between the human organism and cosmic reality, evoking a sense of unity of all of it taken together. Its teaching is that everything that is manifested form arises from totality, making the entire Universe one whole. The ultimate conclusion of the Vedas is known as the Vedanta, which shares that there is only one indivisible unified field of energy or consciousness that underpins the whole of life – one layer of greater cosmic intelligence from which all matter and form manifest – and, wait for it, I am (as are all of you) it. Stay with me here.

Me and the sea

> *The world is one family.*
> – Maha Upanishad –

If you had never heard of the Vedas before reading this book, perhaps you would have heard of the infamous Stephen Hawking who, amongst many other brilliant things, was the modern scientist able to popularise to the greater non-scientific community (to the extent that it was even possible) the scientific field of quantum mechanics.

Quantum mechanics is actually one of the most successful scientific theories of our time. The most illuminating and relevant discovery has been that the Universe is one indivisible field of energy from which all relative things (any form or matter) manifest (whilst always remaining interconnected to their originating source energy field). Was this not what the Vedas had already cognised many thousands of years ago? The connection and synergies between the Vedas and modern science pleased the logical side of my nature.

I am no Einstein, but the way I understand the science is that all of the particles that make up the Universe are not individual and separate balls of matter but rather all part of one giant wave of infinite formless energy. And even when it breaks into individual forms and behaves as if it is many separate parts, it never ceases to be the originating unified field.

I have always wondered why it is so comforting to sit in front of the ocean and contemplate life. I am not one to frolic in the actual ocean often, but I have always been able to retrieve the calm from the calamity when I just sit and watch it. I am a visual bird, and so one particular analogy used by my Guru Spiritual Leader to help me better understand who I am (and those fascinating conclusions of the Vedas and modern science) was elucidating. If you look at an image of a wave breaking from the vast, still ocean, it is so blindingly obvious that, even as it breaks away and becomes a wave, it remains permanently connected to its original source. The ocean. And, not only that, it folds right back on into its vast wholeness after it has played and splashed around on the surface. He used this analogy to help me conceptualise thinking of each physical body on Earth as akin to an individual wave. And then the unbounded ocean (which never stops being connected to the wave) can be thought of as a representation of God, the Source, the Divine (or the whole indivisible consciousness field from which the wave came).

This analogy brought to life some very complicated Vedic and scientific concepts for me. If the curvature of the wave could represent me, Sarah Susak – the individual physical body living a human life on Earth – and the ocean represented the Universe or God – the underlying unified field of all of nature's intelligence – then, just as the wave and the ocean are always connected, I could start to understand and believe that I was also both at all times. Even in my existence as an individual wave or human body, I never stop also being my source.

So, if I am the wave and the sea is the unified field of nature's intelligence – and we are never separate – then, just like that, my sense of who "I" am becomes a lot bigger, a lot more expansive, a hell of a lot more powerful. I started to really comprehend in a practical way one of the main perspectives of the Vedas, which is that individuality is, in fact, also always universality.

After many frustrating attempts to try to crack the code, I got to a point in my life before cancer where I had chucked the mind-bending question "Who am I?" well and truly into the fuck-it bucket. Looking back, I am less sure I did that because the answer was too hard or perplexing, rather because I was just not ready for the answer. Once you have the answer, it renders you almost choiceless but to take advantage of that revelation. To know now that I am more than just my physical body and mind having an individual experience on the Earth's surface – that I am actually also a never-changing, always-present, unlimited field of yet-to-manifest potentiality – delivers me so much liberation from the shackles of the past and so much hope for a more creative and fearless future.

Perhaps even more valuable than the shift in my relationship with who I am, a deeper understanding of who I am *in relation to others* also emerged. It was enough of a mind opener to believe that I personally am never separate from my source. However, the ocean has more than just one wave. All the other waves in the ocean represent other people or things that are around me. And all of them are connected to the same bloody ocean. If I am both Me and the Sea, and if we are always connected, always one, then every other wave (individual) is also the Sea and, thus, Me, too. Even if that sounds like a weird nonsensical nursery rhyme right about now without any rational foundation, you can at least start to see the gift of love and compassion for so-called "others" that this theory of oneness and expanded sense of self can bring.

A special seed began to sprout in my fertile, yet still weed-filled, mind that my relationships with others could blossom more beautifully if I could truly come to understand that every single human being actually comes from the same source. That we are, in fact, just one giant stream of universal consciousness having different individual experiences on Earth. Instead of looking over to other waves of consciousness and comparing myself to them, which creates feelings of inadequacy or fear, I tried to visualise everyone around me as interconnected. I started to try to change my past pattern of divisive disconnects, always ultimately leading to a need to reconnect, and rather focus my future efforts on avoiding the disconnection at all and maintaining peace because, of course, we are already connected.

This truth that there is no such thing as "other" made me start to look at people differently. Everyone around me became a kind of extended self. My capacity to love, be compassionate and have true empathy grew. Me and the Sea and everyone swimming around in it all just started to merge into one, and I started to respect each of our reverential statuses irrespective of our differences a lot more. I sure haven't perfected it yet, and the ego still creeps in to disrupt my love-in vibe, but I am getting better. There is definitely less anger and more peace in my life.

Death is not real

> *None of us are getting out of here alive, so please stop treating yourself like an after-thought. Eat the delicious food. Walk in the sunshine. Jump in the ocean. Say the truth that you're carrying in your heart like hidden treasure. Be silly. Be kind. Be weird. There's no time for anything else.*
>
> – Keanu Reeves –

If you had asked me before I got cancer what my number one fear in life was, the answer would have been immediate. Death. At the time it was not about death of myself as much as it was about the idea that people who I loved might not be with me one day. And it was not just an inability to fathom not having someone I adored in my life anymore, it was the philosophical questions that arose in my mind every time I pondered it. Might sound familiar, but questions like, *well, if we are all just going to die, what on earth is our point in being here?*

There was a time when that idea made me so anxious that I sought professional therapeutic help, and I both laughed and cried when the therapist told me that it was the one fear you could not ask a patient to face by actually experiencing it in order to discover that it ain't all that bad. However, I can tell you that coming up close and personal to not just the mere possibility that I may die but being told that this is a genuinely conceivable outcome brought me about as proximate as I was ever gonna get to an immersive excursion towards the facing of my fear. This was the number one fear that I wanted to get clarity and answers from my Guru Spiritual Leader on, because getting cancer saw it flare up brighter than the Olympic torch, and I could not let it stay alight for much longer or I quite possibly could have melted.

Until I got to this particular juncture in my life, the best I had managed to muster in an effort to overcome the fear was to try my hardest to live my life, even when perfectly healthy and well, with a death-bed mentality. If I knew that I and others in my life were going to die one day, I thought it made good sense to try and approach my life with the mentality that this was an unavoidable certainty and therefore to try to make the most of all moments I had been gifted with.

So, as I faced petty squabbles or questioned whether I should or should not be doing something, after I stomped off to have a big sulk about how wrong they were and how right I was or hesitated to take action due to fear, I would sometimes find the space to quietly ask myself: *on my dying day, is this how I would act or spend my time? What choice would I make then? Would what is bothering me actually matter?* And I would try as hard as I possibly could to make choices based on my answers to those questions.

Some people who I have shared this strategy with have described it as grossly morbid, but, despite its Debbie Downer appearance, I have found it rather useful. In my past my arguments would often lead to soul-destroying battles about who was right and who was wrong, but using the death-bed mentality, I was more capable of transcending the minutiae of point-scoring in favour of protecting the importance of quality time together. And in those moments when something I wanted to try frightened me to my core and I was hovering on the precipice of not doing it, reminding myself that my dying day could be around the corner would propel me back into more courageous laneways.

When I got diagnosed with cancer, I remember hitting a point after a certain number of totally well-meaning sympathetic looks upon hearing my news when I started to think *why the hell are you all busy feeling sorry just for me?* I of course never said this out loud, but I would find myself thinking *hang on a minute, you could actually die sooner than me, even without a cancer diagnosis.* Or the more macabre version: *you could walk out this door after visiting poor little old, possibly dying, cancer-ridden me and get hit by a car or stand under a falling tree.* Are any of us really in a worse position than the other as it relates to dying? I had clearly started to wonder whether it is not, actually, a bad thing to just assume and accept that we can and will die at any time and let that fact lead us in a more positive and less fearful direction.

I can acknowledge that this kind of approach may be a hell of a lot easier to adopt successfully when you are not threatened by a possible imminent death or when nobody you love is nearing their own. Before my aunty Lesley died, I had not experienced the death of anyone in my life who had not died of more natural causes relating to age after having lived a full and graceful life, like all of my dear grandparents when they passed. I am not suggesting that all death is not extraordinarily difficult, but Aunty Lesley died after a lifetime of illnesses which culminated in a terminal brain cancer. She left us well before she was ready to. She died still having so much life and so much potential to offer the world and our family. In those final moments it all felt incredibly unfair.

Lesley encapsulated so many of the qualities I have aspired my whole life to achieve, and she applied them expertly to overcome so many personal challenges. She was one of the first and youngest recipients of a kidney transplant when she was just sixteen years old and died the longest-known-surviving kidney transplant recipient, which summarises her extraordinary capabilities in a nutshell. She had been told at so many times in her life that she only had a defined number of days, months or years left, and each time with her mental willpower and impenetrably strong mindset she defied all those who tried to tell her when her life was going to be over. Even in the week before she died of brain cancer, I referred to her casually in a sentence as sick and she told me she had no idea what I was talking about, such was the stalwart nature of her refusal to tie up her identity or sense of self with any kind of damning or defeatist label.

Regardless of what her body was doing, Lesley kept her mind fresh, her spirit soaring and her perspective laser focused. Doctors had called her a miracle on so many occasions through her life. But those close to her never saw her medical triumphs as miracles. We knew that it was Lesley who had proactively made them happen herself. It didn't feel to us like pure luck; we could see that it was she who was the driver behind the mental wheel at all times, seizing the most out of every moment and refusing to give up.

When I got cancer, she used to counsel me to take it minute by minute, nanosecond by nanosecond if I needed, and just to understand that, right now, I was still here, and that was all I needed to remember and focus on. Such simple words but the ones I remember the most and the ones that carried me through so much of my own catastrophising and fear about the imminency of death during that part of my life.

Flanked up against a history of immense and daily fear of death, through the guidance of my Guru Spiritual Leader on the topic and my growing understanding of the Vedic worldview, I started to become far wiser on knowing how to process and make sense of the enormous pain of Lesley's passing and my momentary escape from death after recovery from cancer.

In those earlier years before embarking on this spiritual path, it was all about grappling with what I had always thought of as an absolute loss, the total eradication and complete cessation of a human being, which of course sounds so extreme is it any wonder I spent so much of my life drowning in depression over the very thought of it. I think I had also struggled with knowing that there is absolutely nothing I can do to prevent its eventuation.

What Thom Knoles' teachings reminded me is that nothing is permanent. Let's face it, from the same minute we are born, we are also dying. The death toll for all humans is 100%. So it had been pretty taxing to my wellbeing up to this point in my life having believed for so long that I was just a mere individual body that once gone, was gone. Learning that I am more than just a physical body and that my higher self is eternal and unchanging got me starting to believe that perhaps when this body, or the body of someone I love, has completed what it came here to do, there remains another part of me (and them) that is immortal. A part that can continue.

Whilst this belief still comes with some relative endings on the surface level of life, it at least provided me with a new perspective. The wave may crash and die, but the ocean continues to flow. As Eckhart Tolle explains it ever so sweetly, we are all actually the Universe expressing itself as a human for a little while. Consciousness itself cannot die, only the body through which universal consciousness is finding expression does. Now, that is still sad, don't get me wrong, but it certainly allows the heavy cloud of fear to lift a little.

I found these spiritual and scientific concepts particularly helpful when grieving my aunty's death. Just like Lesley never thought of herself as sick, she would probably have been even less fond of being known as dead. Who was I to determine the cessation of her experience in our world? And, more so, why would I want to even do that? I could call her dead all I wanted, but there was now a part of me that could conceive and believe that she might well be on her way to a new adventure, a new set of experiences and, better yet, that the Universe may well have needed her indomitable spirit, her sense of survival and her award-winning resilience to lead a more evolutionary purpose for our planet or our generation. I have no proof of this, of course, but while I myself may not like her loss and may feel abandoned or alone without her, to reduce her grandiosity to a mere body no longer felt right either.

All I can hope is that I will see her again sometime soon or feel the effects of her new feats one day in this lifetime and know that it is her. I like to think of this concept now not as a new life after a death but as the continuation of the eternal self (that is immune to death), albeit in a different form. Eckhart Tolle explains it with great brevity in *The Power of Now*: "nothing that was real ever died, only names, forms, and illusions". He describes death as the stripping away of all that is not you and that the secret of life is actually to "die before you die". I understand this as the pursuit of the death of ego, the individualistic self, while one is still alive. What I was discovering with all this new knowledge was that I can actually stay and play forever in "Once Upon A Time" land rather than sit and cry about "The End". How cool is that?

The potential healing power of all of these lessons from my Guru Spiritual Leader seemed to be immeasurable if I could continue to keep my mind open to exploring further some of the spiritual and scientific concepts. I have heard astronauts talk about the life-changing effect of seeing the entire surface of Earth from up in space – how it just appears as one giant whole with no divisions. This felt like it could be that. But how on earth was I to get into space for this kind of perspective without a rocket ship?

PART TWO

Youru

CHAPTER EIGHT

Are You Medi?

We're sitting under the tree of our thinking minds, wondering why we are not getting any sunshine!

– Ram Dass –

Pulling into Meditation Station

Fact is, no scientist is able to "explore" or access the field of pure awareness, the one unified field of consciousness, *physically*. You cannot just walk into no-thing or an invisible energy field. The only way to access that part of who we are is *through our minds*. So, the mission becomes how to achieve access to this fine sounding destination. The Vedas' largest gift to my life was delivered in the form of Vedic meditation – the portal and pathway towards Self-realisation and enlightenment. All the stress and repressed trauma in our lives are impediments to such an awakening. We already have a completely unstressed nature, but our thinking minds are in the damn way.

I mentioned earlier that straight after I got home following all my cancer treatments my anxiety state was incredibly high about the dreaded disease's recurrence. I knew I had to get it under control. And so, heigh-ho, heigh-ho, it's off to Vedic meditation class I go!

The first time I walked into my Vedic meditation class I arrogantly rolled my eyes more times than a pig rolls in a good patch of mud. The juxtaposition of the expensive three storey terrace home it was held in against the more plebeian cushions on the floor for our seating had me instantly wary. My P.E Nation uber luxe metallic tie-dye leisurewear felt somewhat indulgent (and ridiculous) as I sat down cross-legged next to the organic cheesecloth-wearing yogi with her Indian silk shawl keeping her slight and healthy shoulders warm. And I broke all sorts of personal space boundaries just to be able to hear what people were saying as they spoke with their super gentle and quiet meditator voices. Quite frankly, all I wanted to do was scream about how fucked up I felt, but I didn't out of fear of disturbing the peace on all their calm makeup-free faces!

I actually left after Day 1 of my first attempt to learn Vedic meditation. I did the course so soon after my cancer surgery and radiation, and in hindsight I just don't think I was ready. I didn't quit because it didn't interest me. It was my anxiety that prevented me from returning on Day 2. But somehow my commitment to dedicating myself privately to the practice I had learned on the first day continued. I stayed connected to the teacher and the Vedic community more generally. I kept listening to podcasts recorded by leaders steeped in similar knowledge and wisdom. I kept reading books in the genre. And so, in that period between half learning the technique and some of the wisdom of the Vedas, I didn't stop reading, listening, self-learning and practicing. After experiencing more and more, over the course of those years, the benefits of a daily Vedic meditation practice, I am now a Vedic meditation devotee.

Even though meditation is generally taught to you by someone else who purports to know and believe that it is the way, ultimately, once you have learned it, the practice is solitary and invites you to go within, relying only on yourself to continue to awaken. My teacher of Vedic meditation offered me a hop, skip and a jump towards self-sufficiency rather than another dependant attachment that I would need to rely on to bring happiness to me. Meditation was the first practice that allowed me to really believe that self-sufficiency was possible and offered up a technique that gave me direct, first-class access to that reliable, ever-present source of fulfilment within.

The Vedas don't prescribe a set of "rules" or nominate one singular individual who will teach you all about how you should live your life, experience the world and make decisions. Rather, they acknowledge and implore that all of those answers already belong to you. Teachers in this space focus on providing you with a technique that will take you to the more expansive layer of yourself so that you can dip your toes in the blissful waters of pure awareness and see for yourself. And that little rocket ship, now also my BFF 4EVA, is Vedic meditation. The only way towards this larger sense of "self", which the Vedas taught me was, and always has been, present. It is one thing to be told that an expanded sense of who you are exists but it's quite another to know and experience it to be true in a practical day-to-day way. I used to think of my daily practice like an episode of *Perfect Match*, with my individuality on one side of the sliding wall and my cosmic nature on the other, ready to be revealed to one another and become unified in an eternal state of bliss.

When you learn Vedic meditation you are provided with a *mantra*, which translated from Sanskrit means "mind vehicle". A mantra is a pulsation of sound that deliberately has no intentional meaning. The technique does not require you to concentrate on the mantra but rather repeat it effortlessly and silently in your mind until it becomes more and more subtle and your thinking mind becomes less and less noisy and dominant. As that happens you naturally enter that silent state of pure Being and access the very source of all the thoughts that you have now transcended. In this state of transcendence, you are awake and fully conscious but also beyond thought. There is absolutely no effort required to lure your mind away from the outside world of form and phenomena. You just let the mantra do the job. The recommended guidelines for the practice are to meditate for twenty minutes, twice a day, and a good Vedic meditation course will explain the science behind why the practice is taught in this way.

I myself had tried many meditation methods before I found Vedic meditation. For a long time, I was obsessed with guided meditations and concentration meditations (on my breath, on candles, on my body). Both of these techniques were a very useful starting point. The problem I found, however, was that the thought of both sitting down still *and* focusing intently on something scared the always talking, always walking hell out of me. You can imagine that telling someone with a busy, distracted mind to focus on just one thing could seem uncomfortable to them or even impossible. It is also very easy with guided meditations for my mind to start to wander due to memories or associations I have with the words being spoken to me. Whilst it felt good for my body to stop and be still, these techniques didn't give me that escape from my thinking mind that I clearly needed. I also did not deeply understand what it was that I was doing, or why, and so these practices never stuck, and I never saw the benefits long term.

I have had a lot of people tell me that they have tried to meditate and that they did it for two weeks, felt no tangible or miraculous benefit and then gave up. After learning Vedic meditation, there was definitely a self-discipline required of me to build the habit. Not as an off and on exercise that I did only when I felt low but rather an integrated, non-negotiable part of my daily routine. My meditation teacher struck a great balance in holding nothing back about the vast magnitude of benefits of meditation with more realistic guidance around the speed with which they were attainable. Thankfully, as impatient as I am about the idea of any kind of delayed gratification, I was able to see that nothing seismic would come of it other than temporary, sporadic moments of relaxation if I did not make it a part of my daily life. It was made clear to me at the outset that if I was looking for any kind of spiritual quick fix, then don't come a knockin' on the door of Vedic meditation.

Putting a large part of my faith in meditation as a source of survival after cancer, especially to manage some of my fears about it coming back, I was perhaps more determined than the average spiritual seeker. I can see that. But I am proud to say I have barely missed a meditation since I started. I have been known to say I would let my house burn down before I missed one!

I have had meditations where I have closed my eyes and opened them after what I thought was no more than twenty minutes, but two hours had actually passed. In that longer period of time, I had momentarily forgotten about the relative outer world and its concerns, where I was or even that I had a body. Time was irrelevant but it didn't feel like a vacuous state or an absence of anything, it just felt like a beautiful inner contentedness, which drew me back again and again (and again).

One of the biggest reasons I used to believe that meditation was impossible for someone with a mind as active as mine was that I didn't believe there was any way to stop my incessant thoughts. As I learned to meditate and understand the essence of who I really was, I started to comprehend in a more realistic way what people and therapists I had consulted over the course of my life meant when they said that *we are not our thoughts*. I had always believed my thoughts as the gospel truth, like they were the ultimate authority on who I was and the most intelligent and accurate assessor of my performance and capabilities. I still do a lot of the time. Before I learned Vedic meditation, anyone who said to me that I was not my thoughts would just make me have another thought that went a bit like this: *Well, if I didn't think you had no idea before, I certainly do now. How about you just pop inside my chaotic mind space for a day or two, and then you tell me how these bastards are not the real deal!*

But with more and more of the teachings of the Vedas and my continuous daily practice of Vedic meditation, I started to at least entertain the idea that my thoughts were the creation of my ego and past conditioning, and I started to wonder more about this bigger part of myself who was capable of observing those same very thoughts. I now try to focus less on attempts to control and change my thoughts and more on letting them float past my mind, accepting that they are just mere content and not who I really am. And then, to the best of my ability, bin them.

This certainly is not the route of all thoughts that enter my mind, and I still get into mental binds that would make Twisties look like straight lines in comparison. I don't think there will ever come a day when my sense of self is not tied up at moments in thoughts like *I am unwell* or *I am a shit lawyer* or *I am a terrible mother*. But ever since I started to meditate, I have made much more space for an alternative sense of who I am that shares more of the qualities of my source, the unified field. Beliefs such as *I am whole, I am healed, I have unlimited potential* and *there is nothing I cannot handle*. At the very least, if I cannot get to that bigger sense of who I am and the thoughts take over, my level of self-awareness about how untrue or invented those thoughts are helps keep the higher levels of anxiety more at bay, and I am able to recover far more quickly.

One of the most common questions I get asked about my meditation practice is where on earth do I find the time to do it twice a day? What I used to think of as a 2 x 20-minute daily loss became a multitude of gains, the value of which were far greater than the time I initially thought I had sacrificed. In fact, the opportunity cost to my life of not meditating is now far too high for me to ignore. They say that the only meditation to regret is the one that you miss, and I totally understand the meaning of that.

The benefits of Vedic meditation are well researched and well documented. The practice has been proven to provide improvements in sleep, overall health and immunity, reduction in anxiety and depression, greater joy and clarity, and improved focus and memory. Everyone's experience is of course going to be unique, but for me it took a few solid months before I started to herald more health angels into my life as a result of meditation. When I say health, I mean all kinds of health. The health of my mind, the health of my relationships, the health of my body and even just the health of my day-to-day experience on Earth.

I know that meditation is not the panacea to all of life's problems, but the impact of stress on our minds and bodies should not be underestimated, particularly because it is known that stress is one of the highest causes of disease. Our nervous systems were not designed to withstand the amount of wear and tear on our bodies that accumulated stress brings. Think about how many moments of stress can arise during an average day. From children's needs and activities, caring for others, social media and office antics to workload, financial stressors, busy to-do lists and ill health; the list can often seem limitless.

It is not these stressors, though, that do the harm to our wellbeing. Stress is an activation in our body and is more accurately described as the *stress response*. It is our physical and emotional responses to those stressors that dictate the level of negative impact they will have on our overall health state. There is a lot of variability in people's stress responses, dependent on who they are, their age, their background, their level of consciousness, but when we do get stressed our bodies and physiologies change. For example, our muscles may tense up, our breathing could get more rapid or our heart may start beating faster. All of these could form part of a stress response, and they are the kinds of reactions that lead to many of the anomalies in our health and wellbeing. It is the stress response that Vedic meditation helps you manage better. We cannot always change what is happening in our lives, and so it's critical we have the most effective tool to enable us to manage our response to any challenges so that we can adapt and face them in a calm and resilient way.

One thing that I don't think I was quite ready for when I first learned meditation, expecting just pure moments of bliss and absolute stillness every time, was the unravelling of who you are that can also happen. It is a common misconception that meditations must feel smooth sailing and joyful to be counted as good ones. But for a new meditator, there is going to be work to be done on all of the stress, memories and traumas that have been pushed down into their physiology. It has been said that what the mind represses, the body expresses. And so, the internal release of accumulated stress in the body can sometimes make for a perceived "bad" meditation. One that feels uncomfortable or that makes you cry or feel overly emotional during and after you meditate. But the de-excitation of the nervous system that is experienced during meditation allows for the body to start to renovate, heal and release any anomaly that such repression has caused, which can bump the mind back into action. And this is a good thing!

As I started to build my own meditation practice, there was much-needed mental housekeeping that took place intermittently. As I began to quieten my mind, it would occasionally trigger a stress release that would catapult me back into the thinking realm or open up an old wound or fact about myself that I didn't want to deal with (or that was just a plain surprise to me). I eventually came to admit that my history of go-go gadget "doing" and constant high-energy activity was subconsciously to distract myself from facing inner truths, demons and worries which, if remaining trapped in my body, could be super harmful to my health. With more practice, my body and mind felt lighter, as if there was a shift in my ratio of stress to rest, with rest finally being on the higher side.

When this kind of un-stressing occurs during a meditation journey, the number one piece of advice my teacher gave me was not to give up; it means the meditations are working. Our mind and body are connected, and so when our mind quietens, our body does too, which very helpfully activates that part of our nervous system which can focus on renovating some of the harm caused by stress impact. But because of that connection, the activity in our body then bumps our mind back into activity too, until all that stress is cleared right on outta there. So, very calmly, I was advised to just keep on returning to my practice and my mantra, with absolutely no judgement of any of the thoughts and feelings bubbling to the surface.

It's not always easy to just watch a thought flow by and allow it to do so without any self-criticism for having had the thought or allowing it to inspire a second, and sometimes more damaging, thought. But if I ever wanted to be able to successfully manage stress or unnecessary negative self-talk, it became clear to me that I had no choice but to learn how. One of the most instructive tales that I have continuously recalled to help me restrain from layering a negative judgemental thought on top of another thought that arises during meditation, or even just in day-to-day life afterwards, is the Buddhist parable of the second arrow. Its intention as I understand it is to teach us how to deal with suffering more skilfully, which can, of course, include the damage caused by negative thoughts.

If we suffer a misfortune or a have a negative thought, then that thought or that misfortune is the first arrow – which we cannot always control and which, granted, can be painful. But the Buddhist teaching is that the second arrow is *optional* and is just our reaction to the first arrow. I try as hard as I can these days, with the light of more pure awareness from meditation, to catch myself and not to layer my thoughts or experiences with more judgemental thoughts about the initial one. And in meditation, I just do as I am taught and effortlessly return to my mantra.

I learned that the worst thing I could do was to push any negative thoughts that had arisen in my consciousness back into my nervous system and recycle the stress that I was clearly trying to release. And that the thought certainly does not require any more analysis and can simply be observed and then let go of. In one of his teachings, my Guru Spiritual Leader cheekily reminded us that we don't go back to the rubbish bin and yell at it because it has rubbish in it, and that we should be happy that we are starting to remove what is no longer relevant and not to be angry with ourselves but rather try to move on.

Meditation has become the technique available to me anytime of the night or day that enables me to stop seeking. A place that I can visit on my own, and reliant on nobody else, to access unlimited fields of potential and all of the qualities required to navigate life. When I meditate, I drop into this space that is beyond thought and begin to experience and know the much larger and infinitely capable essence of myself. And, in a unifying way, the essence of what others are as well.

All I really need to do every time I feel stressed is remember who I really am and, more so, who I really am *already*. There is nothing to seek or find as it is already there. I am already the ocean, the unified field of cosmic intelligence, which is, of course, already completely fulfilled. What a slice of the knowledge pie to just nibble on for now. What a technique to do anything with but keep up my sleeve. Rather, it must be used and shared with others with wild abandon. This was the start of something special and I knew it.

Cut loose, don't recluse

My perception before I had learned Vedic meditation was that the people who really succeed with and benefit from meditation are monks who retreat into caves and live their lives in silence and stillness. I had never imagined that enlightenment was a goal us everyday householders could aspire to or achieve by making meditation part of our lives. I was worried as I started to learn that so much of my life activity was going to have to cease or at least peel back if I was to truly integrate the benefits of meditation into my overall wellbeing. I have had a lot of people ask me how I do all that I do in my life with my family, my work and other interests and ventures and still stay calm or seem happy. And my answer is always the same – because I meditate. Meditation has not slowed me down at all. In fact, I don't think I have ever made such forward-moving life progress as since I started meditating. The clarity, calm and resilience it brings into my life actually helps me do less and accomplish a lot more.

I think sometimes meditators get a bad rap as being a bunch of hippy la las who wear a lot of white linen, drink chai lattes and, well, don't do that much. You know, they sit cross-legged, chant, chill out, man, and have no worries, dude. I started to notice that people who meditate take plenty of action in their lives, but as a result of the state they achieve in meditation, they go about their regular business in a far calmer, clearer, more productive and blissful state.

It is a common misconception that all meditators are focused solely on establishing themselves in a state of stillness and Being without much Doing. But nothing could be further from the truth. Meditators get to experience the full spectrum of what it actually means to be a Human Being. They get to be Human in the pursuit of achievements and relationships and experiences in the relative, surface world. But at all times pervading that state is the calming and stabling effect of simply Being. A meditator's modus operandi is all about establishing themselves, through meditation, in a state of blissful contentment so that they can then take that state out into the world and continue to take action.

Through my studies I have heard and read a lot of inspiring stories of monks who retreat from community and live an isolated existence in silence amongst forests or on mountaintops and, I am sure, total and utter bliss. I mean who *wouldn't* be capable of that state in that environment? No material things, no relationships, no responsibilities, no constant barrage of social media influencers or advertising, no horrific and terrorising news stories, no expectations and therefore no disappointments or suffering.

This may well be alluring to some, I get that. But for people with desired and satisfying careers, families or other worthwhile commitments, perhaps not entirely realistic. Or, maybe the better way of putting it, for those who like the idea of operating as agents of progressive change out there in the world, not logistically possible. I knew, once I had experienced it, that the baseline inner sense of contentedness and clarity you can reach from meditating was a priceless discovery. But I also felt that keeping it to myself would be of no real utility.

I have come to firmly believe that one of the most divine and important things you can do, once established in that calm and steady state, is to perform right action out in the world – action for the benefit of yourself and all others. As a lifelong Do-er who was now also a tad mesmerised by being a Be-er, knowing that I *could* – and, more importantly, *should* – take action felt like a major life victory.

The inaction we experience in meditation was taught, of course, to be important. It is that very stillness which allows enough de-excitation of the sympathetic nervous system to experience both rest and necessary stress release when relevant. But just as critical is the action we take *after* we have meditated. I did not wish to go into meditation and realise my non-dual, unbounded, infinitely capable nature just so I could live in solitary bliss in denial of suffering that may well come up again in my own life and the world around me. I also had shit to get done.

B.K.S. Iyengar, often credited with popularising yoga for the Western world, once said that the world was already filled with movement but what the world needed was more *conscious* movement. I love that. He called for less *movement* and more *action*, the latter being a term that he described as "movement *with intelligence*". I had always been a bit of a mover and a shaker, but my new calling was to move and shake with intention and from a higher state of consciousness. My mission had become to move myself (and perhaps through my example also others) to greater self-sufficiency. It had become totally clear to me that this could not be done in either total isolation or a state of constant external Guru dependency.

The more times I meditated, the more I returned to that blissful state for short bursts of time, the more my higher state of consciousness (and all of its qualities – of joy, peace, calm, bliss) would imprint itself on my mind-identified much smaller sense of self. This infusion of a more expansive state allows me to take that part of my true nature into my daily activities outside of meditation and, simply, do better. Cue dimmer switch on the darkness in my own life, but also, hopefully, some of the darkness hovering about in a world screaming for greater spiritual sophistication.

There can be no doubt that all of my personal challenges and efforts to seek fulfilment outside of myself had moved me along an evolutionary path, but nothing put me on the starting block for greater personal awakening, greater awareness of the fact that fulfilment was already available, than Vedic meditation. It is the tool with which I became able to start to slowly stabilise some of the chaos, anxiety, fear and tension in my life, and it is the very reason I am able to go back into the world after unexpected change or trauma with a greater sense of capability, self-reliance and joy. With meditation now firmly planted in my life, my earlier struggles towards self-mastery now felt like they could be conquered victoriously.

CHAPTER NINE

Youru

*Guru is not outside; Guru is your own true nature.
Guru is what is looking out of your eyes right now.*

– Krishna Das –

Ahhhhhhhhh. We have arrived. At the greatest and most impactful discovery of my life. Finding Youru through meditation was truly akin to a homecoming. As Thich Nhat Hanh is famous for saying, we don't need a plane or train ticket to go home. I know he is right because meditation takes me there every time. Now is probably a very good time for me to pull my earlier definition of Youru out again. Have another read of it and see if it makes any more sense or has any more meaning for you after coming with me on this journey of my own evolution towards greater self-sufficiency and less reliance on anyone or anything outside. Imagine, when you read it, even if you are yet to believe or experience it for yourself, that Youru is, indeed, you *personally*, and see how it feels to describe yourself in this way.

YOURU noun

(pronounced *you.ru*)

: a universal spiritual teacher.
// The *Youru* found personal enlightenment within and then from that place of inner baseline fulfilment took it to the greater world to share their wisdom.

: an influential teacher of oneself.
// A great *Youru* understands that the most lasting and evolutionary lessons and opportunities for change come from within and not outside of themselves.

: an expert who is popular with themself, first and foremost.
// The *Youru* doesn't seek the validation of other people or things "out there" for their own sense of self-love and from that place can love others unconditionally and with less dependence.

: an especially intellectual guide of oneself in all matters of fundamental concern.
// A *Youru* asks and relies on themself for the answer, understanding that they are the ultimate knower of all things and that it is already within them if they are conscious enough to be aware.

: one who acknowledges themself as the leader and chief proponent of their own life.
// The *Youru* refused to be a victim and give their power away to anyone or any circumstance in their outer environment or postpone their own enlightenment by waiting on it to come from the outer world.

Big Me, Little Me

We have traversed together half a lifetime of Gurus that I have turned to in an effort to remove darkness from my life or to find fulfilment, all of whom bestowed blessings upon me but ultimately never provided me with complete and utter lasting satisfaction. Meaning that if I am not at least starting to move further in the direction of worship of Youru, I could forever remain on the prowl for that one other person or thing that will finally make me happy.

What I hope is that you might have some greater sense now of who the "You" is that I am referring to in this new word and new definition. Throughout my Vedic studies, I have known this larger essence we have playfully conceived as the ocean to be referred to as many different things. The Unified Field, the one indivisible whole consciousness field, Totality or even Nature's Intelligence.

And when used in reference to the fact that you/the individual/the wave are also *it*, the term *Self*, with a capital *S*, is commonly used. This is to distinguish itself from our smaller, individual, localised personality, mind and physical body – that which walks about on the Earth's surface – our (lower case) self. The intention is that *Self* signals the more expansive aspect of who we are, and the source from which our smaller self is derived.

I have always found all of that kind of tongue twisting. You know already about the romance between my heart and the teaching that both self and Self are One, but to keep it simple from here on in, I will start to use two terms that I find much easier to comprehend: Little Me (self) and Big Me (Self). I find this to be the most practical mental construct. At various times when I am acting or thinking in particular ways, I often check in with myself to ask *is it Big Me or Little Me who is having this reaction or experience?* And then make the necessary adjustments if Little Me has taken over where Big Me might see me through to a better outcome.

It is Big Me that is the You I am referring to in the word Youru. And that part of who you are that Little Me needs to find a way to access in order to discover its own independent power.

It is in the presence of Big Me that Little Me is able to finally recognise the qualities she has always had in order to start to truly and self-sufficiently remove darkness from my own life.

In the spirit of Little Me who likes to write stuff down, who likes complex theories distilled into easier-to-digest words, here is a side-by-side comparison of some of the general qualities of each version of who we are. A simple summary. I find it quite powerful.

LITTLE ME	BIG ME
Dependent on others	Self-sufficient
Having a human experience	The Universe
The Wave	The Ocean
Relative	Absolute
Individual personality	Essence
Physical body	Spirit
Form	Formless
The Known	The Knower
Always changing	Never changing
Bound by thoughts	Beyond thought
Ego bound	Ego-less
Temporary	Continuous & Eternal
Conscious	Consciousness
The observed	The observer
Individuality	Totality
Bounded	Unbounded
Limited potential	Infinite & unexpressed potential
Knows what it allows itself to see	Omniscient (knows everything)

In one particular place and time	Omnipresent (everywhere)
Self-doubting	Omnipotent (capable of everything)
Your invention	Your true original nature
Fulfilment seeking	Already fulfilled
Importer of happiness	Exporter of happiness
Separate	United
Lower self	Higher Self
ONENESS	**ONENESS**

How fun to know that you don't actually have to pick a side. That you are not either column A or column B but rather you encapsulate all of these qualities already and all of the time. You just need to know how to access and remember Big Me when your world or thoughts start to narrow in on you. In all honesty, at various points in time as this new information and experience poured into my senses, I had serious moments of resistance, but thankfully my readiness to change defeated my desire to complain. Sometimes our intellect or our ego does not like the problem to be solved or to accept that it is a tad simpler than what we had imagined it to be. I am BIG, problem solved. That can be unnerving to the egoic mind caught up in all its drama.

I can still find myself in a round of musical chairs with both versions of myself, and they are mad little competitors. I can admit that Little Me will still sometimes win a few more seats than Big Me in the circle that is my life, but that's OK. Just knowing that I can bring a greater awareness and try to adapt when Little Me is up to no good or causing harm is comforting. That I can help Big Me score more bums down any time through meditation is also encouraging. What a delight to know that the game of hide-and-seek I had been playing all my life with my own inner Guru could, if I stayed the course with the practice of Vedic meditation, end with one big fat "I fouuuuuuuuuund you."

Recognising there are two parts to who we think we are has enabled me to rely on Big Me more often and, through meditation, seek to employ her greater sense of capability to overcome more of Little Me's false limitations. And, also, to overcome that foolhardy reliance on another Little Me, or Little Me-led idea, outside of my own true nature to bring me the answer I am seeking or some kind of greater happiness. We are not the tiny little bag of hurt, betrayal, issues and pain that we think we are. We are wayyyyyyyyyyyyyy bigger and more capable than that. What we need right now is an advertising agency to create a worldwide marketing campaign for a global online dating app that shows Little Me and Big Me falling deeply in love, with the tagline: "You are the one you have been waiting for."

Know Thyself

As I have said earlier, my relationship with myself is the one that will always be there and likely the most enduring. And so why I had allowed it over the years to be so sub-par bewilders me now. When I was in the throes of that one bad over-and-over-again break-up, one of my best mates and I got matching tattoos. We got the Ancient Greek words *Gnothi Seauton* permanently etched on our bodies. It was one of several maxims inscribed at the Temple of Apollo in Delphi and, transcribed, means to "Know Thyself".

I can put on my big girl pants and admit that, back then, I was probably trying harder to be cool than conscious when I picked that tattoo. But I was definitely in a place of searching as it relates to spiritual support after a broken heart. I certainly did not fully understand the significance of the words I had penned onto my skin forever.

A very wise authority in my life who is a lover of history put it so beautifully when he explained to me that these ancients did not go looking in isolation to find that which made them unique. Rather, they looked for that which they had in common with all people. The goal of their search, he explained to me, was not an estimation of their unique individual presence in the world but rather the birth of community. I have spent my entire life knowing *about* myself, knowing all the individual traits and characteristics, stories and narratives about Little Me. But I had spent very little time, until discovering Vedic meditation, coming to know the true and much larger essence of *who I actually am*.

Knowing who you *actually are* is very different to knowing *about* yourself. Read those words out loud again. I am so pleased to really comprehend the meaning of them now. It makes me smile that well before our time, some thousands of years ago, human beings could see that it was possible to live your life absent of any understanding of who you really are, and they implored people to avoid that error. To *Know Thyself* now carries two meanings to me, having learnt that there is a dual purpose to self-knowledge. One is to assist in making you live your life independent of the opinion of others. But the other is to help you grasp that knowledge and understanding of Self is knowledge and understanding of all others. To Know Thyself is really to create more space for commonality with others and therefore bring more love into your life.

With my discovery of Youru, life became all about relearning and remembering what I already was. We are born whole, unlimited, unbounded. And then from day one, as soon as our little heads pop out and about, all the projections, prejudices, conditions, belief systems and other people's opinions start to put out the flickers of our remembrance of this truth. It is kind of funny to me now that we start out life in a little tiny baby body and we then embark on the process known as *growing up*. This implies that we start small and we grow into something bigger.

This may, of course, be true for our physical bodies and their measurable size. But nowadays I prefer to consider myself as having been born big and then spiralling into a downsizing of that grandness through conditioning. Now all I wanted to do with my time was use it to restore. My whole worldview had changed. Kev Carmody and Paul Kelly wrote the song "From Little Things Big Things Grow". I am choosing to kind of reverse those song lyrics as they relate to my own spiritual development. It is from big things (which is the way we enter this world) that little things grow – *if* we don't remain aware enough throughout our lives to avoid over-identification with our smaller selves. Benjamin Button may well have been onto something. Every day and with every meditation, I get a tiny bit better at not minimising myself and getting all tangled up in my mind-created identity Mademoiselle Little Me (or, worse, the Little Me created through the influence of, or my own reliance on, others).

Before discovering Youru I had not fully understood how very *un*-real my self-imposed deficiencies were. Because of my feeling of lack, I had looked for and pursued happiness and success in places outside of myself. They were always just on their way. Never in my wildest dreams could I have contemplated that all

I needed and wanted to feel was already within me. I know now that the arrival of any kind of fulfilment from out there cannot be relied upon to be everlasting. Non-permanence dictates that such forms of fulfilment will ultimately disappear. These departures (following periods of heavy reliance) can send us into a spiral of suffering. And then on yet another pursuit to *find it* again. No search party is necessary if one remembers who it is they really are and goes within to reacquaint oneself.

I had mistakenly believed, until I found Youru, that I would be somehow made more by my gains or the validation of others. And, worse, that I would be made less if those things I had acquired or the people that loved me were taken away. Totality (my true nature) cannot be made more or less by anything or anyone as it is whole and never changing.

If it is true that consciousness really does become what it sees, then I knew that true change in my life required me to work on moving closer and more often to this higher state of consciousness. And while it was scary to even consider what my life would be like without all of these other Gurus as the source of my confidence, I finally knew that what I now needed was to enthusiastically take my place on the throne of the Guru who has the power to create my very own reality. Me. Little old Big Me.

Be the lighthouse

> *The yogi teaches and serves others in the highest way – by his inspiring life ... Reform thyself and thou wilt reform thousands.*
> – Paramahansa Yogananda –

We often make fun of the classic answer given by aspiring

Miss Universe candidates when they answer that world peace is their motivating aspiration. We really should not scoff at anyone who has an inkling of the need for more peace in this world. But Martin Luther King Jr was dead right when he said that those who want peace need to organise themselves as much, and as well, as those who love war.

Peace won't come into our lives, or the lives of those around us, if we sit around and do nothing about it. It is also a waste of a good life if we wait for others to behave better in order for us to have a better experience. I like to think of any potential positive impact I could have in this world as coming from staying focused on developing and elevating my own state of consciousness. And then maybe, rather than being told how much of a better state of consciousness it is to live in, people would just observe it for themselves from my example. If I seem to be managing the same busy, stressful world that they are, with the same roles, responsibilities and occasional traumas, but with a greater sense of calm and more resilience – then maybe they will enquire with me of their own accord how that came to be.

If, as Youru, we have the power to remove our own darkness, then we can by default be the light that ultimately walks back out into the world to make it feel just a notch brighter. It was now clear to me that any influence I could have to help others move towards greater self-sufficiency had to start with my own personal upgrade. From the lessons learned through my studies and self-work, I now take more deliberate strides to proactively develop more conscious characteristics. To assist not only how I navigate life for myself but also how I show up in the world in a more supportive way for all those special people in my life and, of course, for the wider community.

I am continually becoming aware of things about myself which I know are not quite right. Not wrong, or "bad", but areas for improvement. It could be either in the way I treat myself or the way I treat or respond to others. But now when I get that flicker of intuition and awareness, rather than ignore it and push it down in denial, what I try to do is acknowledge it without judgement then seek to improve it. The characteristics that I have worked most diligently on integrating more into my life since learning meditation have been empathy, adaptive capability and equanimity. I fail a lot but just having the aspiration and witnessing the incremental improvements makes all the difference.

Empathy

I thought I was already a pretty empathetic person before I discovered meditation, but something truly unifying happens when you are taught that every single person, animal and thing is just an extended version of yourself. And just as, through your practice, your field of conscious awareness continues to expand, so too does it widen your everyday sense of perspective. Meditation allows you to move from a contracted to a more expansive state of consciousness. A little bit like spending your life on the balcony rather than the dancefloor. Seeing the world from high up on a balcony, the breadth of your awareness is wide and all encompassing. Down on the busy dancefloor it's crowded and the perspective naturally narrows.

One of my personality pitfalls in the past had been the constant need to prove my point of view as the right one. But now I understood better that neither person's perspective has to be branded right or wrong or better than the other. Imagine for a second there is a number painted on a floor. Two people observe it from opposite ends. One proclaims it is number 6 and the other is certain it is number 9. Who is right?

This analogy is a reminder that each person's unique vantage point – their own individual experience, story, background and level of consciousness – determines their reality. On so many occasions I had taken my own reality as the one gospel reality, which is supremely ridiculous when you really think about it. There are multiple and endless realities or ways to interpret the world around us, all built and configured in our Little Me minds. Knowing now that there really is no universally defined relative world out there but just a variety of consciousness states having human experiences, I started to become less astonished by an alternative conclusion about the same matter by someone in my life. I tried to stop expecting people to act a certain way that suited my particular sensibilities or desires.

Adaptive capability

I have no doubt anymore that new challenges and changes in my life are a given. Rather than trying to inhibit or control the uncontrollable, what I am striving towards now is the ability to have greater adaptive capability in the face of these changes. Almost everybody would have heard of the "fight-or-flight" phenomena in modern psychology. When we are experiencing stress or anxiety, this is the automatic reaction that our nervous systems undergo to get our bodies into a state ready to meet the perceived threat or challenge in front of us. This can, of course, be a life-saving reaction if it is activated so that we can escape from a tiger who is about to have us for dinner. However, it was never intended that we would live a large part of our every day in fight-or-flight survival mode like many of us do in the stress-filled modern world.

When asked about this common response to the trauma of change, my Guru Spiritual Leader invited us to use the practice of Vedic meditation to move further away from *fight-*

or-flight responses to stressors and their negative impact on our longevity and, instead, closer towards the idea that we could build the capability, in the face of a new challenge, to instead *stay and play*. How very romantical of him. But there was something very attractive about being able to have less volatile reactions to change and, more so, a quicker recovery from them.

Old mate Charles Darwin had already made it really clear to us in our school years that our likelihood of survival was directly correlated with our ability to adapt to our environment, but for some juvenile reason I just always imagined that to be true for the lions and zebras and not me. Sometimes real life feels even more brutal than the jungle, and so being able to breathe some truth into the idea that that there is no such thing as a stressful situation, only your reaction to it, felt like it would be a very useful trick of the trade to learn well.

The most illuminating explanation I ever received to help me understand the need to develop a capacity to meet the demands of life more interactively was to think of three different kinds of balls.

First, a granite ball. So strong, so solid, so steady. Seemingly unbreakable. But definitely breakable with the right masonry tools and the right amount of heavy pressure applied. It is quite common for some humans to display the same stoic, seemingly unaffected reaction to stress, much like a granite ball on its first hit from the hammer. Humans who push down deep beneath their outwardly tough exterior all their emotions that they do not want to face or try to release. But more often than not, just like the granite ball, if enough pressure is applied or accumulated, these kinds of people ultimately reach a breaking point.

Second, a ball made from modelling clay. It is malleable and can be shaped in all different kinds of ways. But once moulded, it is completely unable to revert to its original shape naturally and of its own accord. Representative of humans who are likely to experience a permanency from the impact of external stress and, just like a clay ball, are easily shaped by their environment.

Finally, the glorious foam rubber ball. The foam rubber ball is just as malleable as the clay ball but with the admirable quality of resilience. Once this ball is squished by outside pressure, it just calmly and almost immediately resumes its original shape after the pressure has been removed.

All of these balls had the same stressor of the human hand upon them, but it's the rubber ball that had the least permanent and least violent reaction to that stressor. The rubber ball was able to meet the challenge of being squished momentarily and recover quickly, returning to its full repertoire of behaviours very easily. All hail the rubber ball. I certainly plan to channel my inner rubber ball in the face of whatever may come my way next.

I know that I can never avoid stressors in my life, that is just plain Disney-like thinking. I will never stop *getting* stressed or feeling it deeply, but I can at least stop *staying* stressed for inordinately long periods of time. I can learn to recover faster, reducing the cumulative and negative effect of stress in my life and body and for those around me.

Equanimity

Stress reactivity and the reduction of its harmful effects if not managed well felt more achievable the more I came to grasp and practice equanimity. This is a fancy word which essentially describes the ability to maintain an evenness in your mind regardless of circumstance. This is not just about staying calm in the face of crisis but equally relevant to the ecstatic, overly excitable states that I am well known to overtly display over joyful moments, achievements or acquisitions. The latter is less about any dulling of the senses or reducing any enjoyment of nice experiences, achievements or things and more about not getting into such elevated states of excitement over someone or something that could be removed from my life as quickly as it entered.

Funnily enough, I still find it much easier to maintain equanimity in the face of a loss than I do in the face of a gain. Over-enthusiasm is my middle name. However, when good things do happen, I have now been taught that it isn't about making like a foam rubber ball but rather an oak tree. The late and great Thich Nhat Hanh made the observation that "When we shout at the oak tree, the oak tree isn't offended. When we praise the oak tree, it doesn't raise its nose." I mean, c'mon, if you don't wanna praise the lord, I am good with that. But not praising me? I am not sure I can even try getting jiggy with that. I love a bit of praise. I love getting it and I love giving it. And profusely. I could spread a dollop of praise mayonnaise on just about any moment. If my eight-year-old daughter uses a coloured pencil in a mildly creative way, say to draw two straight lines, I tell her that she is the most talented child in the Universe and that her art is akin to Pro Hart. If I do a load of washing (and fold it) and my hubby doesn't tell me what a good wife I am? Sad face.

Forget about bountiful and exaggerated praise in response to achievement for just a second. What about maintaining equanimous stability in the face of an acquisition? Watch me click a "Purchase Now" button (or, worse, when the SMS beeps that says "your delivery will be arriving today"), and you will see what a totally non-equanimous reaction looks like. Or witness the spiritual nosedive from equanimity I take into TOTAL FURY when I've chosen "leave it in a safe place" – to deliberately shorten the time and space between me and that new thing – and that same SMS informs me that I was not home, so they took my delivery to the local Post Office. It ain't pretty.

If such great importance is placed on their existence, one only needs to experience a reduction in praise or the loss of a new purchase, and feel the resultant fall from grace into suffering, to know that there is an element of truth here. Mastery of greater equanimity was clearly of great importance if I wanted to take my place more squarely in a zone where cycles of losses and gains of people or things outside of myself could no longer make or break me.

I do not wish to lose my sense of enthusiastic passion and joy, ever, but recognition that this kind of inflated reaction could actually be harmful was an important thing as a parent and aspiring Youru to wrestle with. Being unshakable in the midst of all the outer world activity or, at the very least, less impressionable or distracted by the joy or the sorrow of the senses would mean that I was closer to understanding Big Me as already whole and eternally safe and blissful.

Truth be told, just like the beautiful lotus flower which rises in bloom above its own roots that are grounded in muddy water, we too can experience growth, beauty and life even when stuck in the mud. We just need to come to know Youru and continue to try to grow our own capabilities. Finding Youru, for me, has become less about seeking relief from life and all of its challenges and more about acceptance of all of it. It has become less about retreating into unitary solace giddy with the knowledge I was gaining and more about growing as an individual and developing the kind of human characteristics that may bring more light into the world. And then, most importantly, sharing that with the world. That kind of self-work is now part of my every day and always will be. As my Guru Spiritual Leader so elegantly said, you cannot be the light of the world if you cannot pay your own light bill.

CHAPTER TEN

Comm-Unity

Kings and philosophers shit, and so do ladies. Even on the highest throne in the world, we are seated still upon our arses.

– Michel de Montaigne, circa 1580 –

Sandwiched between a rock and a judgemental place

In the dizzying heights of young ambition, I used to make my way proudly from Town Hall Station into the concrete tower jungle of lawyer land for my very first job as a paralegal. Every day, I would walk the same route past a Woolworths supermarket and notice a man with a cardboard sign that begged total strangers for help. His head was sunk in a state of dirty shame, and he never looked anyone in the eye. I made the silent judgement that so many people make – that giving him money was not helpful and that he may just spend it on alcohol or drugs. And so, instead, I would buy him the same McDonald's Happy Meal and simply drop it in front of him on the ground each day as I passed.

I did that for some months. Not once did I say hello. Never did I ask him who or how he was. I just gave him the meal and gave myself an arrogant pat on the back. Popped a few more dollars' credit into my imaginary karma bank and continued on my merry way towards the big shiny office. One day, the man set fire to the brown paper bag with his lighter and threw it at me.

As I turned around, furious, about to publicly berate him for his lack of gratitude, he just stared me down. He looked me straight in the eyes, for the first time, and asked, "Did you ever stop to think that I might want a fucking salad sandwich?"

Oh lord have mercy for the shame that hit me in my face faster than I could hurl any insults towards him. Humbled by his courage and embarrassed by my judgement, that day was a massive turning point in my evolution towards the importance and power of community. I believe that community is one of the foundational platforms that enables people to get to Youru with more surety and speed. But, also, the very thing that one should immerse themselves in once they have established themselves in that state through meditation. It is truly where I believe an elevated state of consciousness, one of love and compassion, can make the most difference in the world. So, on that day, I sat with this man. I truly met him. And I started my own journey towards relinquishing more of my judgement of others in the spirit of greater unity.

There is no doubt that if there was a medical term for a "helping others" gene, I was probably born with it. From my early days in the schoolyard right through to the stressful workplace and into the broader community, I have always extracted the most joy out of each place by figuring out how being there meant I could help someone. To learn, then, as I did through meditation, that all these "others" were extended versions of me and that I am eternally connected to them has made the experience much more important and meaningful, increasing my motivation to keep it up.

Even before I learned these unifying concepts through my spiritual development, I found that to volun-teer always left me feelin' a whole lotta volun-cheer. I have talked a lot in my life about how community giving is as selfless as it is selfish. What it is that you give, or sacrifice, in order to help someone else is often totally and utterly trumped by what you get back for yourself from having connected with and learned from that person.

Honestly, many of the people I have met through my charitable work have enriched my life and influenced who I am today more so than people I interact with in my day to day. I have always been inspired by the saying that the true measure of human character is how you treat those who can do absolutely nothing for you. In a somewhat divisive world where the chasm between the fortunate and the unfortunate often feels inordinately wide, growing up I had always been taught to treat everyone the same. From the office cleaner to the CEO, from the person on the street to the person in the mansion.

In my earlier years, living life with this attitude felt more about advancing basic human equity and plain old good manners. As I got older, it shifted to a more established and deeply held belief that none of us are actually any different. And now, knowing truly, madly, deeply that we are all, in fact, One, the unity in community started to feel even more attainable. And so violently important to strive for in a world so divided by conflict and opposing points of view.

What had held me back in the past from being able to truly live this way was that unconscious, and often deadly, judgement that is made when you look at someone else and their life choices. All around the world, we see human beings making judgement calls about people who do not share their worldview or customs. One does not need to look far to witness the shattering impacts of this kind of intolerance and the need to find ways to contribute to its dissolution.

So, after being reprimanded by this gentleman on the street for my unhealthy, no-option food donation, I made it my personal mission to get to know and understand better as many people living on the streets as I could. I started doing outreach walks on the street at night with a group of people from the Wayside Chapel known as the "Shepherds of the Street", to connect with young people living rough without a home. The Wayside's mission is to create a community with no "us and them", by providing love, care and support services to people experiencing homelessness and social isolation in the local area, and it didn't take long for me to fall in love with and dedicate myself to this worthy cause.

The more involved I got, the deeper I wanted to dive. I started to sleep as a volunteer one night every week with those taking shelter at a run-down old chapel in Kings Cross, led at the time by the glorious Father Steve Sin (I mean, could you get a more ironic yet rock star name for a priest?). I would commune with the other visitors, listen to their stories and share my own, and make sure they were fed and felt looked after and secure about having shelter that night. The resources were incredibly thin, and by "shelter" I mean the church floor with sleeping bags. On those Friday mornings that I made my way from that old church floor directly to a fancy legal office, I am sure that people wondered where I might have been as I was too much of a pansy to shower in the public toilets and had slept in fairly unsanitary conditions. But I made so many beautiful friends and connections there, and these evenings became some of the fondest memories in my life.

I started to spend more and more time volunteering at Wayside. I did most of my shifts in the early days in the community cafe or community services centre talking to all of the eclectic visitors. I started to really take the time to get to know these beautiful people, whom I had previously circled around with a wide berth, and sought to understand even just a smidgeon of their daily experience more deeply. The thing that struck me most back then, but that makes a whole lot more sense since experiencing the benefits of consciousness expansion in meditation, was the importance of staying aware of context if you want any chance of maintaining a dose of perspective when the chips seem down in your own life.

The wider your knowledge and understanding of what the world is like for people beyond your own contracted band of experience or exposure, the greater your sense of perspective will be. You start to remember that broader context when the victim narratives begin about whatever it is you are going through, and all of a sudden it doesn't seem so bad. A little bit like that saying which wisely counsels that somewhere, someone in the world would just kill to have your problem. It is a commonly used retort to complaints made about something that is a seemingly small problem relative to someone else's – that the complainant clearly needs to *go and get a little perspective*. It can be very hard to understand that kind of feedback, though, when stuck in your own narrow palaver pothole.

Helping others, truly taking the time to get to know their story, their experience and their point of view has widened, and continues to expand, my context and understanding to a point of greater unity. And has allowed me to see some of my own problems in a different and perhaps more favourable light. There is a whole lot of truth in the adage that if you want to feel sad then think only about yourself, but if you want to feel happy then think of others.

I can look back now at my very early beginnings as a community volunteer and acknowledge that my ego was getting in the way of making a true connection with the visitors who were there. I spent so much of my time stuck in a kind of hero complex, trying madly to fix everyone and make them better according to my standards and expectations of the world.

I will never forget a penny-dropping experience I had on one particular outreach volunteer shift. I left this memorable shift in an awe-inspired state after taking so much personal learning from the Wayside staff as they went about executing on the chapel's promise to see everyone as a person to be met, not a problem to be solved. The precise rationale for working with this philosophy was so that their efforts could unify rather than separate. How nice would it be if we thought about all the relationships in our lives in this way? These community service workers did not try to make the people they met during the outreach more like them, they would rather just be alongside each of them on their individual journey.

For every person on the street or in the community housing that we visited, I wanted to provide a job offer, a material necessity or a connection to someone who could solve their problem. It was almost like I had to sit on my hands and tape up my mouth as I watched in awe the social workers' ability to do and dream exactly the same things for the people that they so clearly loved but rather allow the individual to initiate that journey at their own will or pace. They never even contemplated imposing their own worldview on what might make these people happy or fulfilled. They were so acutely perceptive of what was appropriate for each person and what was not and almost chameleon-like in their ability to show and express love in just the way each person needed on that day.

They knew not to push practical solutions on the anxious man who clearly was comfortable in his place that night as a victim. They knew how to deliver food and clothing with just the right level of equanimity so as to take care of the father of three's pride at not being able to provide that week for his family. They could laugh with glee along with one man's obviously substance-induced joyful ecstasy, delivering just the right balance of playfulness and no judgement with loving advice and guidance on how to self-care. They would take indignant action at the atrocious news from one man that his children had been sleeping under a leaking roof now for nine months and vowed to work with community housing to correct that unfairness.

It was so clear that the pain and joy of those they visited was also their own. What I was witnessing in the cold, hard light of day, wide awake and very conscious, was the gift of unity that community service delivers. I am exceptionally grateful for the personal evolution I have experienced from the very first day I was invited into this precious cavity of community.

So many people have asked me how to get more involved in community, and I always tell them the same thing:

Find and identify the cause or the issue that means something to you. If something specific doesn't naturally spring to mind, then start to take note of how witnessing suffering and injustice, or, conversely, how being immersed in creativity and innovation, makes you *feel*. Pay attention to what makes a sadness well up inside or your blood to boil every time you see it. Observe what makes the hairs on your arms stand passionately on end or tears of happiness roll down your face. Once you are aware of any of those feelings inside of you, it means you care. It means it matters to you. It means there is most definitely a call to action from nature for you to be involved somehow or part of the solution. It could just be that who you are and what you have is needed to serve others.

Follow your intuition and reach out to an organisation that exists in the area that has you lit up inside or caused you to bawl your eyes out to see if there is some way you can support its cause. Guaranteed, they need you. Guaranteed, they will have a role for you to play. Don't just cover your eyes and ears in the hope that their issue or charitable pursuit will go away or progress on its own. Or assume that one person cannot make a real difference. You have to take action and try.

R.I.P Tommy

There is not a more commonly known saying than you should never judge a book by its cover. Quite simply because if you do, you might miss out on one of the best reads of the year. Same goes for people in the community, I say. Putting any form of judgement of what we can now safely term so-called "others" onto a one-way removalist truck to rid any form of it from your worldview is what I would call a very, very smart move. I am proud to say that I had one of the best life teachers of the value of this human quality, one that allows for the building of greater peace and unity. His name was Tommy. I feel like it is so important for me to put down in words the story of my time with Tommy. I feel driven by the need to honour the important life, and very existence, of a homeless man who became one of my greatest friends.

When I first met Tommy on the street, he told me that I had "nice pins". Tommy was extremely intoxicated at the time, but what was meant (on my part) to be a five-minute chat to be polite turned into a five-hour marathon conversation with that very same man. I can admit that it is so incredibly hard not to let all your own beliefs, opinions and assessments come into your mind when you witness people in states so far removed from your own. But, boy, did meeting Tommy fast track my graduation from Judge Judy to Masters in Community Service.

Tommy had just one bag with him on that day, other than the brown paper one he clung to a hell of a lot more tightly than he did his suitcase. If I am really honest, it was Tommy's suitcase, and the isolated manner in which it accompanied him, that captured me at first. I was mesmerised by the nonchalant way he had left it a hundred metres away from him without any surveillance. This complete disconnection to what appeared to be his only worldly possession fascinated me.

In a way that I was not consciously aware of at the time, I was Pandora and Tommy's suitcase was my box. Curious, I asked him what was in it, and suddenly a territorial instinct rose up in him to protect this once-abandoned bag. I was informed that, in spite of my delightfully long legs, there was no way I was getting inside that bag. Which, of course, only made me want him to open it even more. When I eventually flashed just enough leg to encourage him to prise it open, its mysterious contents, a wealth of unexpected information, unleashed another wave of shame over my inner (and bloody arrogant) predictions on what would be inside.

What struck me first was the sentimentality of the belongings. In my juvenile beginnings as a community service afficionado, I had expected to find whatever rags he had picked up off the street to wear, old food bits kept spare for a hungry night and, at best, one or two pictures of what was once his life. But the first thing Tommy unravelled from the stories contained in the bag was a photocopy of a lottery ticket and a clearly aged and ragged article from about him from an old newspaper.

Tommy had actually won the lottery a long time ago. As is often the case with lottery winners, this point in time was both a blessed pinnacle and a horrifying damnation for Tommy, of which, naturally, he could not have foreknown. At the time when this little pot of gold was placed at the end of Tommy's rainbow, it was considered to be a lot of money. A potentially life-changing amount.

Tommy's rainbow at that time included his children, his wife and, as he put it to me, his simple but happy life. As Tommy tells it, unfortunately the financial winnings brought him no happiness at all. What he had taken to be a ticket to freedom for him and his family ended up as a greedy act of betrayal: his wife allegedly pocketed the winnings and took all of his kids to live abroad. I know every story has two sides, and I was only privy to one. But something in the way he told his tale made me trust that it was true.

I pass no judgement as to how this all happened or why. The detail of importance is that Tommy was once just like any one of us. In a family, probably with some suffering, but more or less happy and with absolutely no intention to ever live a life on the street. He could literally have been me or any person I know that had experienced a life blow.

I was in the early stages of my career when I met Tommy but stayed friends with him throughout as I moved up the corporate ranks. Because the law firms I was working for were all based in the city, where Tommy was known to wander and inhabit, I started to meet him regularly. At his request, I gave him a phone, and I would often spend my weekend days perched upon a milk crate with Tommy and his street mates, all just talking, sharing and solving the world's problems together.

I remember in one such gathering being struck by meeting a man who, I was later told, was once an esteemed and eminent-in-his-field doctor who became gripped by alcohol and pain medication. He would take my pulse every time we met but never spoke to me. It was clear that just allowing him to hold my wrist and remember for just a few beats who he was and what he loved before he became homeless provided him with some comfort. And it served for me as a powerful reminder that every single one of us, even those who feel we are higher up on a sturdy and particular throne, are actually just one stone's throw away, after an unexpected misfortune, from this kind of disadvantage.

What followed for Tommy and I were many glorious years of one of the most unique and engaging friendships I have ever had. We would meet often for lunches and he would come into the city to pick up free personal care products that the company I worked for graciously allowed me to gift him. At one point, after much consultation with his social workers, my then partner and I even provided him with a rental apartment that we subsidised together and fitted out for him with all the typical yet basic mod cons. I will never forget the day that he was found in an intoxicated state in that apartment. We had no choice, as a term of our agreement with him, which the social workers advised was important for boundaries, but to ask him to move out. Which, of course, saw him make his way back onto the street.

He and I spoke a lot about why, when given that opportunity to have shelter, he could not maintain the behaviours required to secure that safe spot. In the end Tommy had become so used to the freedom that he believed came with living life on the street. He used to counsel me that the way us other people went to work every day in the same office, working long hours with high stress, bingeing on TV shows at night and then getting up to repeat it again and again was not what he wanted for his life anyway.

I remember him telling me that he enjoyed marching to the beat of his own drum and that maybe he had a thing or two to teach me about liberation also. Regardless of which way you cut it, neither one of us was, in fact, right or wrong. We can never know when we look at a person what their story is, what put them in the place that they are now in. And we must never judge or forget a person's original nature as the source of all Being. Just like, and, in fact, no different at all to, ourselves.

Tommy died many years after I met him. I am sure in part as a result of his alcoholism. When he passed, there was no one to afford him the right kind of farewell, as is the case for so many homeless people. I will be forever grateful to my own mother who went ahead and arranged his funeral and buried him in a proper cemetery with his own tombstone on my behalf. I was unfortunately living and working in Paris when he died and far too far away from home. I would have liked to have been there when this happened, but it just wasn't possible. My mum was, in fact, the only person in attendance at his funeral. If we had not organised this for Tommy, he quite simply would not have had a funeral at all. He would have left this world without any acknowledgement. This was just not something my mother and I were willing to bear.

When Tommy died, the police had nowhere else to go but to my unexpectant mum's home because he had listed me as his next of kin, I believe, with the department of social services. Given that I was living overseas, you can only imagine the moment of instantaneous fear my mother experienced when two policemen knocked on her door and asked her if she was my mother!

Looking back, walking alongside Tommy for so many years, watching him go in and out of consciousness states and all of his choices (that were so different to ones I would have made) crystallised for me that people are constantly changing and evolving. And so, to label them as any one thing, be it a loser, a homeless, an addict, a nobody, is just not OK.

But it is not just as simple as not judging people and accepting them as they are. It is also about celebrating all people for what they can become. When I find myself in judgement of another now, I try not to be so short-sighted. I try to remind myself that I was not always as delightful as I think I might be now. And that everyone around me has the same potential for infinite evolution and growth if that is what they ultimately choose. And if they don't, or if their personal evolution is a tad slower than my own, can I not love them anyway?

In the end, Tommy was not really homeless anyway, because he always did and always will have a home in my heart.

CHAPTER ELEVEN

From Drama to Dharma

*Try not to become a man of success,
but rather try to become a man of value.*

– Albert Einstein –

What's my Dharma?

One of the most regular conversations I have with people in my life is about them not knowing what their passion is or what it is that they were "meant to do". I mean, I have had the same conversation with myself many a time. The other recurring and more troubling dialogue is often about that universally felt heavy burden that comes with spending the largest portion of our time, 8 hours a day for 5 days (and often more) a week, at our jobs and not at all loving how it is that we spend those precious hours. Every time I talk about it with people who are really, truly stuck, they often say, "But I have no passions; I don't know what it is that I like or that makes me feel good. I have no freaking clue what my purpose is." I have come to see real patterns in these conversations over the years. The knowledge I have acquired from studying the Vedas and meditation has really helped me compute those patterns and understand how to tackle them better.

In many ways, what I have learned has debunked many of the myths and misconceptions about the topic and has elevated me out of the drama that comes with continuous efforts to solve this seemingly unsolvable and deeply unsatisfying problem. There is a delightful concept in the Vedic texts, *Dharma*, which according to the Hindu traditions means to live your life in attunement to, and in accordance with, the laws of nature that govern the Universe. Without getting too technical, it essentially means moving towards finding what it is that is *your personal role in the evolution of things.*

Once coming to understand this concept, I started to think of pursuit of "purpose" less in the context of what it is that Little Me thinks that I should do with my days or how I should earn money and more in terms of how Little Me can operate as a physical and productive outlet for what Big Me feels that the world needs right now.

After learning more about Dharma, I realised that I had been over-intellectualising the concept of purpose far too much. I have a tendency to be too prescriptive and limiting in my understanding of what each human's individual purpose needs to be. Which often leads to stagnation and just making no choices at all because I don't feel the level of certainty that I have it right enough to take any risks.

But even after learning that my purpose could be as simple as to work on expanding my awareness, to evolve and grow, I was still left with the haunting question of *how on earth am I meant to know what it is that will help me do that?* Before I found Vedic meditation, I was led, largely, by what I called the "goosie" test. If something gave me goose pimples or made my arm hairs stand on end when I was out and about, having a conversation or just watching a movie, I would take a mental note and try to remember that this was possibly a good indicator that whatever I was hearing or witnessing could indeed be one of my passions.

Too often we tend to write off these sparks or intuitions

because we deem the actions prompting the feelings "not serious enough" or insufficient to make a living out of. So, if a miserable investment banker got all the feels when they observed the flickering light on the leaf of a tree they passed, but they couldn't see how money could be made from that particular love-in, should they then just park it as something they took only momentary pleasure out of? Of course, it could just be a deep respect of nature, but it could equally be the start of a happier future leading an environmental protection organisation. Or what if you literally cannot stop watching comedies, and only comedies, obsessively on Netflix because it brings you so much joy and happiness and relief from the sad day you have had in a job you hate? Sure, it may just be an enjoyable and much-needed segment of escapism and down-time. But what if it could also be an indicator that you should volunteer at a charitable organisation that has a mission to bring cheer to sick people?

While my goosies remain a valuable source of information from my senses to identify where my passions (and thus purpose) might lie, I gotta tell you that, my twice-daily twenty minutes of meditation, and all the wisdom that comes with it, started to reduce my need to attempt to intellectually figure it out at all. Now, when in doubt, I go deep within myself and touch on that layer of self that is all-knowing already.

Accessing the more subtle impulses of nature's intelligence in meditation, I am able to expand my state of awareness to turn down all the noise and inputs from the outer world. When I head back into my day, I find that I am able to stay more aware of, and better interpret, those subtle impulses and what my desires seem to be guiding me towards.

I think sometimes one of the biggest inhibitors of the pursuit of that which you know deep down to be desirable can be the misconception that your Dharma has to be your career goal or your day-to-day job. And, worse still, that you can only have one purpose for the rest of your life. This can make it feel far too scary to take the first step, for fear that if you do and you do not like it, you are somehow back to where you started. But Dharma, according to the Vedic worldview, does not just mean your duty or your job.

Dharma is what you need to do, right now, in this moment only, to meet the need of this very specific time both for yourself and for the world. This means that your Dharma is not a static thing fixed for all time but can change constantly according to whatever it is the Universe needs you for. Knowing this helps me move more quickly and neatly back to the present moment and significantly narrows the field of the previously giant "what should I do with this life" question down to just this singular moment.

I believe that even if you are in a job purely as a result of the need to fund your life, that is OK. You can still find a way to derive purpose in a place that you know is ultimately not what you want to be doing long term. Even if, with time, you start to lack the desire to climb the corporate ladder right to the top, maybe your purpose there could be to lead people in a way that helps *them* develop or grow personally and professionally. If you look hard enough, you can find purpose anywhere.

But Dharma is not necessarily your job, so let go of that idea right now.

This helps reduce the fear and loathing that comes with trying to decide what to do with the rest of our entire lives. Truth is, you don't need to pick just one thing and do it forever ever. Nuh-uh. And you don't have to be linear about it either. I have always disliked the question in job interviews about where I see myself in five years. Now I know why. If living your life in Dharma merely requires to you to become aware of and strive towards addressing the need of a particular point in time, meaning right here, right now, how can you possibly predict what that highest need will be in five years' time?

I have found this so liberating. And in so many ways, before even discovering this fundamental truth, I had been sorta kinda experimenting living in this way already. When I chose very early on in my life to study law, that decision was led partly by the desire to show certain people from my past that they could not bring me down and that I would succeed and partly by a strong innate sense of the need for social justice in a more philosophical way. However, in later years, the drive for that kind of corporate career was more motivated by other factors.

Once I'd transitioned from private practice law firms to becoming an in-house lawyer, the subject matter thrilled me and the intellectual challenges kept me well on my toes. There were new problems to solve every single day and no monotony, and that suited me. I also enjoyed the salary that reduced my life stress, especially when raising a child, and the position fulfilled my passion for leading and mentoring others who were about to embark on a similar career path.

At different points in my working life I have pondered questions quietly in my mind. Like why had I chosen to be a lawyer in a corporate setting – a setting that sometimes felt like it was not quite where I belonged – and what my personal contribution to it was. In some ways I liked the idea of taking what I had observed over the years of the parts of corporate life that I found unnecessarily tough or harsh and seeking to influence that culture in a more meaningful or kinder direction.

However, there was one particular juncture in my legal career, when it was flying as high as I ever thought it would, when the need of the time called me to do something completely unexpected.

Up, up and a-Wayside

I was just twenty-nine years old and working as an expatriate legal director within a large global multinational living in an all-expenses-paid penthouse apartment in Paris, smack bang in front of the Eiffel Tower. I was responsible for the company's legal affairs in many countries across Europe, Africa/Middle East and the South Pacific, with a clear path towards working on Park Avenue in the New York head office in a global role with the iconic toothpaste company Colgate-Palmolive.

This was undoubtedly one of the best jobs I have ever had, and on the face of it I had no real reason or conscious desire to ever leave it. Life in Paris was nothing but grand. More annual leave than seems legally defensible (love the Parisians), four-week stints in chateaus with friends from all over the world joining me, jet setting every weekend to another part of Europe, Eurostars to London whenever I wanted to see my besties. I cannot lie, the location and the lifestyle made for a fairy tale. Bike riding along the river Seine, shopping on Avenue Montaigne, sipping bellinis on sidewalk cafes in Le Marais. The only thing I would say is that perhaps I was feeling a tad lonely and isolated. I hit a time in my life where I knew that my yearning to start a family was strong and the clock was tick tick ticking.

Truth be told, I have always felt like there are two versions of me, each wanting to pursue a different career – one in the for-profit sector and the other in the not-for-profit or wellbeing world. The former fulfilling my ambitious, academic and intellectual side and love for pace. The latter speaking to my love of helping others. It is almost as if I am not a happy person if I am not doing both.

I remember the call that I received from the then pastor of the Wayside Chapel. He told me that the future of the organisation – one that I had such love for and history with as a volunteer for such a large part of my life – was being seriously threatened by a lack of major funding. I became transfixed with being part of the plan to ensure that it remained a sustainable and long-term part of the community. It had reached a stage and age where they were really needing to attract new corporate partners and major donors, and they thought that my passion for community combined with my network and knowledge of the corporate world would lend a hand towards their goals. He invited me to apply for a job back in Sydney as their partnerships and fundraising manager.

Obviously, the job came with a very modest salary, a mere smidgeon of what I was earning as a corporate lawyer in Paris. It was also a job that I literally had no formal education, skills, qualifications or experience for. Sure, making the decision to actually do this probably did put at great risk my ability to return to the legal profession (and, boy, did a lot of people feel the need to share that opinion with me at the time). Don't think for one second that I just acted with reckless abandon and had no fear for what this meant – including a move back to Sydney from Paris. But, for me, the risk of potential regret from not meeting this higher momentary need was far greater.

And so, after some online interviews from Paris, and with my gut instinct that this was right firmly intact, I hopped on that plane. I let go of my grand salary and lifestyle and started what remain three of the best years of my life serving the community and raising much-needed money for an organisation I love and for people who needed me. I didn't realise it then, but what made this decision flow with such ease was because I was acting in accordance with the need of the time and remaining relevant to the larger evolutionary process. Sure, it was bloody scary and feelings of sadness for what I was leaving behind swelled up inside of me, but in doing so I learned that it's OK to be sad about making the right decision too.

The best part of this story is that after several glorious and purpose-filled years of providing that service to the community, I received an unsolicited call from another of the world's biggest global brands privately recruiting for a general counsel. The calling back into the legal profession came at the precise time I was about to embark on IVF to get pregnant, which is an expensive exercise. And so, the timing was equally divine. All those fears I had faced about not being able to return, and especially to a role that was exciting, were unnecessary and abated.

I did not give up Wayside all together. I joined their board for the next six years and had the great pleasure of being able to serve the side of me that liked to help others while also addressing the side of me that wanted to lead change in the corporate world. At my request, Coca-Cola, my new employer, also allowed me to serve on the board of their Coca-Cola Australia Foundation, which afforded me that much-needed balance I was after between corporate Sarah and philanthropic Sarah. The lesson: take control over the choices you make and the changes you ask for when it comes to how you spend your working hours. You don't have to fit a mould, and it's OK to have dual desires and dual purpose. Make them known to those around you and take proactive steps to find a way to incorporate all your interests into the one working week. It is possible.

There were times in my legal career when I gave a lot of thought to where it was, specifically, that I wanted to practise law. You might bag your dream job and be loving it, but then the structures, cultures or people surrounding you might change. And if that happens and it does not feel right anymore, the answer does not have to be to arrogantly hate and berate those changes (which, believe me, I wasted a whoooooooole lot of precious time doing after a particular corporate restructure), but rather to accept that it is *you* that might have changed.

The light-bulb moment in my efforts to work out what to do when the changes arrive was the realisation that it is fruitless to continue to point the finger at anyone or anything and rather just accept that it is probably likely that one's own personal experience and perceptions have simply changed. So, when I experienced a sudden shift from flying high to feeling like a fish out of water where I was, the answer was not to bring my own confidence house down and stay where I felt alien. Nor was it to continue blaming it on the rain. Rather, the answer was to find a new environment to flourish in again. One that was more aligned to my *current* needs and values, and one that really needed my specific and unique skills and strengths based on its particular stage of growth, which is exactly what I did.

I interviewed at many global FMCG companies and had some wonderful and exciting offers and opportunities to consider. But this time I took great care and patience to find the role that was truly right for me. I was very happy to find a position as general counsel at Australian food manufacturing company Kinrise. They make delicious food that is all made in Australia with iconic family brands such as Greens and Cobs. In this role, I was as close as you can get to the decision making and had autonomy but was also part of a very close-knit team. It suited me to a tee. Lawyer Sarah felt happy and settled. But community Sarah kept a watchful eye and conscious awareness on her constantly evolving Dharma.

Medi Steady Go®

Yogasthah kuru karmani
(Established in Being, perform action)
– Maharishi Mahesh Yogi –

Medi Steady Go® is now my own personal formula for the cycle of my daily life. And, I am thrilled to say, also my business name. In addition to being a corporate lawyer, I am also a passionate teacher of Vedic meditation, and it is an honour to share this critical technique for living life well.

I **meditate**, twice, every single day to connect to Youru, to establish myself whenever possible in transcendence of the ego and my thinking mind. With this practice, the benefit of greater emotional and life stability unfolds, and I am able to **steady** myself as I leave meditation and successfully re-enter my day-to-day activities, challenges, interactions and constantly changing outer circumstances. With every repeated meditation, that stability becomes a more dominant aspect of my nature, and a calmer, more resilient, more peaceful, more empathetic person continues to evolve. As this personal strength solidifies, I then **go**, confidently, out into the world with an intention to perform action – conscious, intelligent, loving and right action – for the betterment of myself and all others.

After I learned it myself, I felt compelled to bring Vedic meditation to the world. One of the great benefits of meditation is that when you reduce the constant and chaotic noise of the thinking mind, you actually create space for clear, conscious, focused decision making. All of a sudden you are more capable of "doing it all" because you are less flustered and therefore more efficient. And so, my new Vedic meditation teaching business was formed, and I am sure it will continue to evolve. The foundational principle or inspiration behind starting this business was a beautiful Sanskrit saying "Yogasthah kuru karmani", which translated means "Established in Being, perform action".

In the Vedic worldview there are seven states of consciousness available to everyone seeking greater enlightenment. They are taught in my meditation course in detail, but one of them is reached during meditation: a state where you are fully conscious but not thinking – you are awake but have transcended your thinking mind and accessed that layer of your consciousness that is pure Being. Then the next state is when you retain this state of Being whilst simultaneously engaging in activity out in the relative world. Meaning that even when you are busy living your life as Little Me, you are still aware of your true nature as Big Me. Being in this state while out in the world allows you to perform action that is of benefit to the entire collective. It is not about only establishing yourself in a state of Being; it is about taking that state back out into the world to perform right action.

Could the Vedas have offered up a more perfect life mission for someone who was never going to give up all the doing which she found so damn enjoyable but who wanted to do it without all the stress, calamity and overwhelm? And from this discovery sprung forth the name of my business, a business and a Dharma which enables me to offer something in service of the broader community.

I want to be the kind of meditation teacher who openly shares my personal history and story and who fully understands the lives my students lead. Lives that they don't always want, or have the ability, to turn their backs on. So, I developed a course that incorporates all the knowledge and wisdom of the Vedas, maintains the purity of these ancient traditions and teachings, but added a little bit of my own flavour to really connect well with students who are seeking fulfilment out there but need to know, quick smart, that what they are seeking is already within them. They just need to learn how to access it.

At the end of the day, I love letting my Dharma guide my decisions about how to spend my days on Earth rather than my small, often misguided and indoctrinated ego. Eckhart Tolle offered me a way to truly conceptualise the meaning of this wisdom when, in his epic book *A New Earth*, he explained that when you can come to accept and experience that we are One with all of life, you also come to realise that it is not you that is living your life but rather life that is living you. "Life is actually the dancer. You are the dance." Not the other way round.

I tell myself now not to worry if I ever feel like I am on the prowl for signs about what it is that life is wanting me to do in any given moment. Instead, I just do my best to stay as conscious and aware as possible, and if something takes my fancy, I just dip my toe in and try it for a while. I am more trusting of the intuition that arises from the daily practice of meditation and allow myself to give things that I feel charmed to do a shot, even if it turns out to be just momentary and not eternal.

These days, as I get up each morning, I take a second to check in and ask Big Me *what is it that she needs most right now? What is it that I can do today to leave this world a better place for having been here?* She does not always answer immediately, but that's OK. I close my eyes, meditate and kick her ass into gear again.

Epilogue

When all is said and done, more is said than done.
– Lou Holtz –

In the prologue I started pontificating about the lack of joyful outcomes or guided direction towards self-sufficiency that nursery rhymes offer us. We started with Jack and Jill, the sailor who went to sea, five little monkeys and good old Humpty Dumpty. All with such dismal outcomes. But before I sign off from this epic discovery that I hold the power to remove darkness from my life, I realise that I would be remiss to leave out Sir Black Sheep. It's always the black sheep that gets overlooked, isn't it? But in all his baa baas, Sir Black Sheep, when asked if he had enough wool, didn't ask for more. Nope. He was enthusiastically clear about having – and being – more than enough already. Three bags full, in fact. But he didn't stop there, the legendary furry mammal that he is. In all his glorious wisdom and acknowledgment that nothing more could ever make him more whole, or fulfil him more than he already was, he also took action. And action for the betterment of others. One bag for the master. One for the dame. And, bless his sweet soul, one for the little boy who lived down the lane. I mean, c'mon. Could you sum it up any better? Word.

Afterword

For so many years, since I was quite young, I have said the words "I have a book in me." Whenever somebody asked what it would be about, I would just shrug. When I reflect on that simple and unsubstantial reaction to the question (with the 20:20 vision that comes with hindsight), I can see that it was *au contraire* to my personality at that time to have that kind of casual nonchalance about goals. And yet, not once did I berate myself for inaction or lack of clarity the way I have been known to do when a desire to achieve a goal has bubbled its way to the surface of my never-satisfied mind.

I have lived my life, until finding Vedic meditation, being driven by my desires and then consumed by all the doing that comes with pursuing them. In fact, as desires came to life and were then fulfilled, I would, out of my need for more, proactively go out of my way to seek out a new desire to achieve in order to fill my now desireless cup. If, dare I even fathom it, a desire was not met or, worse, was met but only short lived, my fulfilment factor always went down a few notches.

So, in the light of what I know now, what, then, was this consistent, unsolicited feeling and deep desire I have had for almost half of my life that there was a book in me waiting to come out? Despite many, many years of having the desire and not even attempting to understand why, let alone fulfil it, not once did I say to myself *clearly it ain't gonna happen, smarty pants or you useless fool, you are all words, no action*. Why, unlike with every single other desire I have ever had, did I not seem to care as much whether it happened or not? Subconsciously I think I just always knew that it would happen, one day, when it or I was ready. And this meant that I was completely unattached – for one of the first times in my life – to it actually coming to fruition. This was so unlike me, but I did not clock that back then.

When I started to write this book, I was perplexed again by what I was labelling for a while there as apathy or laziness because I was not in my usual rush to reach my goal and instead engaged in writing spurts whenever it felt good to do so. Whenever I did decide to write, it flowed effortlessly. After finishing writing the first draft, I learned more about desires from the Vedic perspective and came to understand that this seeming indifference I was feeling was, in fact, evolutionary. Accidentally evolutionary, mind you. But I'll take it.

In this particular teaching, I learned that deep desires are always owned by Big Me and are felt and experienced by Little Me precisely because they are what is needed for a greater evolutionary purpose. I could never have been made more by a desire to write a book. Nor could I be made less by not completing it.

I am, after all, already limitless. Without even knowing it while it was happening, my entire experience and attitude towards deciding to and then writing this book was a living, breathing practice of the spirit of this learning. Fulfilment of this particular desire by Little Me was quite simply the name of the game. My role was to fulfil the desire of Big Me, not to seek to be fulfilled by the desire itself.

To live life in the way that I used to, to continuously seek to acquire new desires or idle in unnecessary quandaries about whether a particular desire will bring me joy or suffering is, in fact, missing the entire point. Big Me is always in organising mode, and Little Me cannot be made any bigger or smaller by a mere desire. A desire is a signal to you that you are needed. That you hold the power for progression not just for yourself but for everyone around you.

The Treasure Chest

Where there is ruin, there is hope for a treasure.

– Rumi –

A creative and inspirational charity CEO that I know, who writes weekly stories to the community, once said to me, after I praised him for some wise words he had written, that he had never had an original thought in his life. He was deadly serious, but I also know he was just being humble because he was, actually, abundant with wisdom. But something about it really resonated with me.

I get asked for recommendations of inspiring books or podcasts or knowledge courses all the time. I get it. We are all in search of that golden answer. We know, of course, that knowledge is power, and different points of view and perspectives can be so enriching.

The Treasure Chest is the curated culmination of years of collection and research. Some of the treasures in this chest have helped me form my own world views and have been a lifeline when I was finding it hard to cope. When challenges in my life arose, my natural reaction was always to inhale knowledge. And it sure did serve its purpose. I would read, listen, absorb, seek to understand, reject what didn't resonate and use what made perfect sense. It's nice, though, now to know that the richest treasure and the deepest knowledge are also already within me. We need not rely on these resources, but they can be terrifically helpful as you embark on or continue your own journey towards discovering Youru. Enjoy the trove!

Books

A Brief History of Time, Stephen Hawking

A New Earth, Eckhart Tolle

Ask Jules, Jules Robinson

At the Feet of the Master, Jiddu Krishnamurti

Autobiography of a Yogi, Paramahansa Yogananda

Ayurvedic Healing: A Comprehensive Guide, David Frawley

Be As You Are: The Teachings of Sri Ramana Maharshi, David Godman (editor)

Beat Cancer Kitchen, Chris Wark, Micah Wark

Becoming Supernatural, Joe Dispenza

Be Here Now, Ram Dass

Brahma Sūtra Bhāsya of Śankarācārya, Swami Gambhirananda (translator)

Breaking the Habit of Being Yourself, Joe Dispenza

Brief Answers to the Big Questions, Stephen Hawking

Buddha's Brain, Rick Hanson, Richard Mendius

Catching the Big Fish: Meditation, Consciousness, and Creativity, David Lynch

Chris Beat Cancer, Chris Wark

Creating Affluence, Deepak Chopra

Creative Visualization, Shakti Gawain

Deep Hope, Diane Eshin Rizzetto

Dying to Be Me, Anita Moorjani

Emmanuel's Book: A Manual for Living Comfortably in the Cosmos, Pat Rodegast, Judith Stanton

*Everything Is F*cked: A Book About Hope*, Mark Manson

Factfulness, Hans Rosling, Ola Rosling, Anna Rosling Rönnlund

Growing Yourself Up, Jenny Brown

Heal, Kelly Noonan Gores

How to Starve Cancer, Jane McLelland

Ian Gawler: The Dragon's Blessing, Guy Allenby

In Love with the World, Yongey Mingyur Rinpoche, Helen Tworkov

Keto for Cancer, Miriam Kalamian

Leaves of Grass, Walt Whitman

Letting Go: The Pathway of Surrender, David R. Hawkins

Life After Death: The Burden of Proof, Deepak Chopra

Love and God, Maharishi Mahesh Yogi

Mahabharata: The Greatest Spiritual Epic of All Time, Krishna Dharma

Maharishi Mahesh Yogi on the Bhagavad-Gita, Maharishi Mahesh Yogi

Manual of Healthy Longevity & Wellbeing, Luigi Fontana

Oneness With All Life, Eckhart Tolle

Outrageous Openness: Letting the Divine Take the Lead, Tosha Silver

Perfect Health, Deepak Chopra

Paths to God: Living the Bhagavad Gita, Ram Dass

Polishing the Mirror Ram Dass

Quantum Body, Deepak Chopra

Quantum Healing, Deepak Chopra

Radical Remission: Surviving Cancer Against All Odds, Kelly A. Turner

Revolution, Russell Brand

Science of Being and Art of Living: Transcendental Meditation, Maharishi Mahesh Yogi

Siddhartha, Hermann Hesse

Solve for Happy, Mo Gawdat

Still Here, Ram Dass

Super Brain, Deepak Chopra, Rudolph E. Tanzi

Super Genes, Deepak Chopra

The 5 AM Club, Robin Sharma

The Alchemist, Paulo Coelho

The Anxious Generation, Johnathan Haidt

The Artist's Way, Julia Cameron

The Bhagavad Gita, Eknath Easwaran (translator)

The Biology of Belief, Bruce H. Lipton

The Body Keeps the Score, Bessel van der Kolk

The Courage to Be Disliked, Ichiro Kishimi & Fumitake Koga

The Courage to Be Happy, Ichiro Kishimi & Fumitake Koga

The Happiness Trap, Russ Harris

The Healing Self, Deepak Chopra, Rudolph E. Tanzi

The Monk Who Sold His Ferrari, Robin Sharma

The Path to Longevity, Luigi Fontana

The Portal, Jacqui Fifer, Tom Cronin

The Power of Now, Eckhart Tolle

The Prophet, Kahlil Gibran

The Ramayana: A New Retelling of Valmiki's Ancient Epic, Linda Egenes, Kumuda Reddy

The Secret, Rhonda Byrne

The Seven Spiritual Laws of Success, Deepak Chopra

The Seven Spiritual Laws of Yoga, Deepak Chopra

*The Subtle Art of Not Giving a F*ck*, Mark Manson

The Three Questions, Don Miguel Ruiz, Barbara Emrys

The Tibetan Book of Living and Dying, Sogyal Rinpoche

The Untethered Soul: The Journey Beyond Yourself, Michael A. Singer

The Upanishads, Eknath Easwaran (translator)

Think Like a Monk, Jay Shetty

Training Wheels, Amy Naylor Haible

Transcending the Levels of Consciousness, David R. Hawkins

Transitions: Making Sense of Life's Changes, William Bridges

Upside: The New Science of Post-Traumatic Growth, Jim Rendon

Up Until Now, Petrea King

Wellbeing Begins with You, Yuan Tze

When the Body Says No, Gabor Maté

Working Identity: Unconventional Strategies for Reinventing Your Career, Herminia Ibarra

You Are the Placebo, Joe Dispenza

You Are the Universe, Deepak Chopra, Menas Kafatos

You Can Conquer Cancer, Ian Gawler

Podcasts

Agents of Wellness, Natasha Mason/Nourish Melbourne

Oprah's Super Soul, "A New Earth" 10-part series, Oprah Winfrey, Eckhart Tolle

Essential Teachings, Eckhart Tolle

Know Thyself, André Duqum

On Purpose, Jay Shetty

Slow Mo, Mo Gawdat

The Mindvalley Podcast, Vishen Lakhiani

The Vital Veda Podcast, Dylan Smith

Vedic Worldview, Thom Knoles

Courses

Exploring the Veda with Stephanie Colman, www.stephaniecolman.com.au/exploring-the-veda

Mastering the Siddhis with Stephanie Colman, www.stephaniecolman.com.au/mastering-the-siddhis

Medi Steady Go® Vedic meditation course with yours truly, Sarah Susak, www.sarahsusak.com

The Zen Academy: Create an abundant conscious business with Tom Cronin, www.tomcronin.com/zen-academy

Vedic Meditation Teacher Training with Tom Cronin, www.tomcronin.com/meditation-teacher-training/

Documentaries, movies & talks

Awake: The Life of Yogananda (Amazon Prime Video, Gaia)

Heal, www.gaia.com/video/heal

The Portal, www.entertheportal.com

The Social Dilemma (Netflix)

"The way we think about charity is dead wrong", Dan Pallotta (TED talk)

UnCharitable, www.uncharitablemovie.com

Wild Wild Country (Netflix)

Support

Carla Wrenn (naturopath), www.peninsulaherbaldispensary.com.au

Dr Alice Nguyen (chiropractor and kinesiologist), www.awakenlifenow.com

Dr Ben Panizza (ear, nose and throat (ENT) surgeon), https://completeent.com.au/profile/ben-panizza/

Dr Dan Rowe (hand & plastic surgeon), www.drdanrowe.com.au

Dr Eve Tsironis (best GP in the world), www.cammeraymedicalpractice.com.au

Dylan Smith (Ayurvedic practitioner and holistic health educator),
www.vitalveda.com.au

Gidget Foundation Australia (mental health support for expectant, new and potential parents),
www.gidgetfoundation.org.au

Jes Chev (Ayurvedic treatments, herbs and meals),
www.jeschev.com

Jéssica Sippel (massage therapist),
@jsippeltherapies

Lifeline,
www.lifeline.org.au

Olivia Shurdova (acupuncturist and energy healer),
www.consciouswellbeing.com.au

Rebecca Cuskelly (clinical psychologist),
www.theprac.com.au

About the Author

Sarah Susak is a full-time working mum.

A commercial lawyer with over two decades of experience, Sarah has led the legal function of some of the world's most iconic brands, including Coca-Cola and Colgate-Palmolive, across the South Pacific and Europe.

In 2017, shortly after becoming a mother, Sarah was diagnosed with a rare and deadly head and neck cancer. Her journey through major facial reconstructive surgeries, intensive radiation treatment and ongoing medical challenges led her to discover the ancient practice of Vedic meditation, which became a cornerstone of her recovery and inspired her to train as a Vedic meditation teacher. In 2023 she launched Medi Steady Go®, a business dedicated to sharing the wisdom and techniques that she credits with saving her life.

After being in remission of cancer for almost seven years, while completing *YOURU* in 2024 Sarah was diagnosed with a metastasis to the lung. Though safely removed, she developed a rare autoimmune condition which saw her on life support and hospitalised for almost three months. With the help of holistic health practices and her daily meditation routine, she made a remarkable recovery, defying medical expectations.

She is now living a joyful and purpose-filled life in Sydney with her husband and daughter.

YOURU is her first book.

@sarah_susak | sarahsusak.com

www.ingramcontent.com/pod-product-compliance
Lightning Source LLC
Chambersburg PA
CBHW060555080526
44585CB00013B/577